LORENZO DE' MEDICI
Selected Poems and Prose

LORENZO

DE' MEDICI

Selected Poems and Prose

Edited by Jon Thiem

*Translated by
Jon Thiem and Others*

The Pennsylvania State University Press
University Park, Pennsylvania

Library of Congress Cataloging-in-Publication Data

Medici, Lorenzo de', 1449–1492.
    [Selections. English. 1991]
    Lorenzo de Medici : selected poems and prose / edited by Jon Thiem;
    translated by Jon Thiem and others.

        p.   cm.
    Includes bibliographical references.
    ISBN 0-271-00772-9
    1. Medici, Lorenzo de', 1449–1492—Translations, English.
    I. Thiem, Jon.   II. Title.
    PQ4630.M3A6   1991
    851'.2—dc20   91–7756
                                                                        CIP

It is the policy of The Pennsylvania State University Press to use acid-free paper for
the first printing of all clothbound books. Publications on uncoated stock satisfy
the minimum requirements of American National Standard for Information Sci-
ences—Permanence of Paper for Printed Library Materials, ANSI Z39.48–1984.

Frontispiece: Lorenzo de' Medici, attributed to Antonio del Pollaiuolo (fifteenth
century). Courtesy of the Národní Galerie, Prague

For Barbara

Or qui lingua o pensier non par che basti
a intender ben quanta e qual grazia abbonde,
là dove quella candida man tocca.

CONTENTS

PREFACE

When, fresh out of graduate school, I first read Lorenzo de' Medici's "Ambra" in Italian, I felt the thrill of discovery. A new poetic world opened before my eyes. More than any other Florentine writer I knew, Lorenzo succeeded in capturing the beauty, seasonal changes, and rhythms of life of the Tuscan countryside, the stage setting for his Ovidian myth about the nymph Ambra and her narrow escape from a passionate river god. I wondered why I had heard so little of Lorenzo the poet, and why "Ambra" and his other long poems had never been translated into English. Only much later did I find answers to these questions, which concern the curious vagaries of Lorenzo's reception history and are dealt with in part III of the Introduction. On reading more of Lorenzo's works, I encountered a body of untranslated poems containing vivid evocations of the natural world, enchanting mythological tales, and lively, often humorous stories of everyday Tuscan life. And so in 1977 I began the project of translating Lorenzo's neglected masterpieces.

This is the first book-length selection of Lorenzo's literary writings to be offered in English. Though renowned as a statesman, politician, and patron, Lorenzo is hardly known in the English-speaking world as the major poetic voice of the Florentine Renaissance. Appropriately, Lorenzo will be making his debut in English on the eve of the quincentenary of his death (1492), and at a time when much of the world will be celebrating Renaissance Italy as the progenitor of the Columbian discovery of America. I hope this selection of Lorenzo's literary writings, along with the interpretation of them in my introduction, will serve as the basis for a new appreciation of Lorenzo's achievement. I also hope that it will give pleasure to students and general readers, and allow them to experience firsthand an ebullient expression of the Florentine Renaissance, without which our understanding of the Quattrocento remains one-sided and incomplete.

Because of intervening projects and other duties and commitments, this selection of Lorenzo's literary writings is somewhat less inclusive than I had originally intended. I particularly regret not having had time to translate a "Wood of Love" in its entirety. The book at hand is, nevertheless, the fruit of fourteen years of persistent, if often interrupted, research, reading, textual study, lexicographical inquiry, translation, revision, and retranslation. As a result I have accumulated a thousand debts of gratitude, of which I can acknowledge only a few here.

Deans Loren Crabtree and Tom Knight were unstinting in their support of the project through the College's Professional Development Fund. They generously provided funds not only for typing the manuscript but also for research trips to Europe and the purchase of books. Over the years, Rosemary Whitaker, the best of Chairs, has done a great deal to advance the project, granting me a sabbatical leave, allowing a lighter teaching load at one crucial point, and generally clearing away many little obstacles that stood in my way.

Patsy Boyer and Elizabeth Leister generously gave their time to read through the introduction. Through their valuable suggestions they saved me from many, though not all, infelicitous expressions. To the late Rudolf Gottfried I owe a great debt for his detailed criticisms of the translations themselves. His early encouragement convinced me that the project was indeed worth doing.

The first book-length study of Lorenzo's literary writings in English, by Sara Sturm, appeared in 1974, not long before I began these translations. Her study proved to be an indispensable guide and later a valuable touchstone for my own critical approach to Lorenzo. I am also grateful for her active support of the project.

Through the years the project has received generous encouragement from friends and colleagues around the world, among them Charles Ross, William Kennedy, Valeria Conte, John Ahern, Sarah Lawall, Will Johnston, Gary Ianziti, Gertrud Champe, Dennis Kratz, and Patrick McCourt. I am particularly grateful to Gerry Soliday for his enthusiastic support of the project from its inception, and to my teachers Willis Barnstone and Edoardo Lebano, who awoke and fostered my interest in literary translation.

Among the many individuals who helped me find books or track down art works, I would like to single out Evelyn Haynes, Emily Taylor, and Joel Rutstein, all from Colorado State's Morgan Library; Pier Luigi Renai, who acquired several important studies for me in Italy; Claire Renkin, for her expert advice on Renaissance art history; and Daniel Ladislav from the Národní Galerie in Prague for his help in securing the rights to reproduce a photo of the Prague bust of Lorenzo. I am also indebted to Hazel S. See-bode's generosity in giving me a rare copy of her late husband's translation of Lorenzo's "Commentary," along with permission to use parts of it.

It is a pleasure here for me to acknowledge the helpfulness of my colleagues at Colorado State University, especially Betsy Berwanger, Paola Malpezzi Price, who advised me on many a crux, Tom Mark, Mary Crow, Carol Cantrell, Ward Swinson, and Bob Hoffert.

For her unselfish assistance and sustaining support throughout the eventful years of this project, I owe the greatest debt to my wife, Barbara.

ACKNOWLEDGMENTS

The editor wishes to thank the Národní Galerie in Prague for its kind permission to reproduce a photograph of the bust of Lorenzo de' Medici by Antonio del Pollaiuolo.

Grateful acknowledgment is also made to the following for permission to reprint excerpts from the works listed: Biblo-Moser, Cheshire, Connecticut, for *An Anthology of Italian Poems*, translated by Lorna De Lucchi. The Putnam Publishing Group, New York, and H. Levtow and M. Valency for *The Palace of Pleasure*. Phaidon Press Limited, Oxford, for *The Life of Michelangelo*, by Ascanio Condivi, edited by H. Wohl and translated by A. Sedgwick. Macmillan Publishing Company, New York, for *Literature of the Italian Renaissance*, by Jefferson Butler Fletcher. Mrs. Hazel S. Seebode for *The Comment of Lorenzo de' Medici*, translated by Murray Linwood Marshall.

CHRONOLOGY

1449   Lorenzo de' Medici born in Florence on 2 January to Piero di Cosimo de' Medici and Lucrezia Tornabuoni.

1454   Begins studies in Latin and Italian with Gentile Becchi.

1459–62   Begins humanistic studies with Cristoforo Landino, Giovanni Argiropulo, and Marsilio Ficino.

1462   Birth of the Platonic Academy at Careggi, under Ficino.

1464   Death of his grandfather Cosimo, *pater patriae*. His father, Piero, becomes ruler of Florence.

1465   First diplomatic mission, to Milan. First version of "The Partridge Hunt" (1465–68)?*

1466   More diplomatic missions. Lorenzo takes a more active role in Florentine politics. Period of the *brigata*, Lorenzo's band of friends, including Luigi Pulci, Braccio Martelli, and Sigismondo della Stufa, all mentioned in "The Partridge Hunt." Cf. also Letter 1 (1463). He falls in love with Lucrezia Donati, the young daughter of a patrician Florentine family. She will be the lady in whose honor he competes in tournaments; she will also be the object of his platonic love in the sonnets and in "A Commentary." First lyrics of his canzoniere? First version of the "Symposium" (1466–67)?

1469   Wins first prize in a tournament dedicated to Lucrezia Donati. Marries Clarice Orsini, member of the powerful family of Roman nobles, in a political alliance rather than a love match. Death of his father. Barely twenty-one, Lorenzo becomes head of the Florentine state. "The Novella of Giacoppo" (1469–70).

1470   Consolidates his political position in Florence (1470–71). Latest date for the composition of "Nencia of Barberino"?

*The dating of Lorenzo's literary works is often approximate and uncertain.

1471   First child, Piero, born. Attends coronation of Pope Sixtus IV
            in Rome; collects marble statuary and precious gems and
            cameos.
1472   Initiates the reopening of the University of Pisa. The town of
            Volterra revolts and is sacked, apparently against Lorenzo's in-
            tentions.
1473   Capitolo 6 of "The Supreme Good." Completion of the "Sym-
            posium" (1473–74). Earliest sections of "A Commentary on
            My Sonnets" (1473–78)?
1474   Tensions between Lorenzo and Pope Sixtus IV. Alliance be-
            tween Milan, Venice, and Florence. Capitoli 1–5 of "The Su-
            preme Good."
1475   Birth of his second son, Giovanni (the future Pope Leo X).
1476   Latest possible date of "The Partridge Hunt." Composition of
            the dance song "Oh lovely woman" (1476–77).
1478   The disgruntled Pazzi family, backed by Pope Sixtus IV, con-
            spires to overthrow the Medici by means of assassination.
            Lorenzo's brother Giuliano is killed, but Lorenzo escapes. Sup-
            ported by the people, he succeeds in further consolidating his
            position. Sixtus IV and Ferdinando of Aragon, King of Naples,
            declare war on Florence.
1479–80   With Florence doing poorly in the war, Lorenzo makes a dan-
            gerous secret visit to Ferdinando of Aragon in Naples, his en-
            emy, who finally agrees to peace, having been won over by
            Lorenzo's boldness and eloquence. Triumphant return to Flor-
            ence and further consolidation of power. From now on, ac-
            cording to Guicciardini, Lorenzo is virtual lord of the city,
            whose democratic institutions now exist in name only.
1481   Two more assassination attempts against Lorenzo, both foiled.
1482   Lucrezia Tornabuoni, his mother, dies.
1483   Congress of Cremona, where Lorenzo distinguishes himself as
            a diplomat. Gains prestige as statesman and peacemaker.
1484   Pico della Mirandola arrives in Florence. Poliziano tutors
            Lorenzo's children. Installation of the new pope, Innocent VIII,
            who will support the Medici. War to capture Sarzana from the
            Genoans; only Pietrasanta taken. Further work on "A Com-
            mentary" (1484–86)?
1485–86   Lorenzo becomes the pivotal figure in maintaining the balance
            of power in Italy, particularly after his successful mediation of

the "War of the Barons" between Pope Innocent VIII and King Ferdinando in Naples. His diplomatic efforts are decisive in maintaining peace in Italy and keeping out foreign aggressors until his death.

1486   Latest possible date for the "Corinto," probably composed in the mid-1480s. Earliest date for the "Ambra"? Earliest date for the "Woods of Love," probably composed between 1486 and 1492.

1487   Conquest of Sarzana.

1488   Death of his wife. Marriage of his daughter Maddalena to the son of Pope Innocent VIII.

1489   Lorenzo recalls Savonarola to Florence and intervenes with the pope on behalf of Pico della Mirandola. "Song of the Cicadas." More work on "A Commentary" (1489–91).

1490   Works with Pico and Poliziano on assembling a large library, the future Laurenziana. "Song of the Seven Planets" and "The Triumph of Bacchus and Ariadne." Writes the Prologue to "A Commentary" (1490–91).

1491   His religious play, "La rappresentazione di S. Giovanni e Paolo," is performed in Florence.

1492   Accord between Innocent VIII and Ferdinando of Aragon, mediated by Lorenzo. His son Giovanni named cardinal. Afflicted by uricemia, Lorenzo dies on 8 April at Careggi.

INTRODUCTION

I

Lorenzo de' Medici (1449–92) so typified the *uomo universale* of the Renaissance that it is helpful to speak of two Lorenzos— one the politician, the other the poet. As Machiavelli said, "You saw in him two wholly different persons, united in an almost impossible union" (979).[1]

Lorenzo was at once a man of action, who shaped the political climate of Italy, and a man of letters, whose writings reveal a keen observer of his age. Intimate as he was with most of the rulers of his time, he seemed to prefer the company of poets, philosophers, and humanists. On the one hand, he was the virtual ruler of Florence, head of the powerful Medici bank, and the leading Italian statesman of his time. His policies helped to establish a delicate political equilibrium throughout Italy and to maintain the independence of Tuscany. On the other hand, he was a major Quattrocento writer, author of a large and various body of poetry and of an important literary treatise, who was instrumental in renewing the vernacular literature of his age after a period of stagnation.

At times, the "almost impossible union" of these two persons could produce impressive results. Lorenzo's literary accomplishments helped in a variety of ways to further his political interests. From the political perspective, his literary activities can be seen as a significant part of a broad program of cultural diplomacy, which also included "loaning" Florentine artists to other city-states (Elam 816–20), sponsoring spectacular public festivals, and providing a wide range of support for humanistic studies. One powerful justification for the political aims and methods of the

---

1. Unless otherwise indicated in the footnotes or Bibliography, the translations into English are my own. In this passage, from the *Istorie Fiorentine* (see the Bibliography), Machiavelli is actually addressing the split between the serious and frivolous sides of Lorenzo's personality.

Medici was the cultural pre-eminence of Florence in Italy and the world. And no one was more adept at publicizing this superiority than Lorenzo himself.

Thanks to his literary gifts and his superb humanistic education, Lorenzo was able to present himself as the finest embodiment of Florentine culture. It was not just that his status as an accomplished poet and man of letters lent prestige to his reputation as a statesman. Much more, Lorenzo could play the role of the enlightened ruler, whose prototype was Plato's philosopher-king. In an age that witnessed the revival of classical learning, and of Platonic studies in particular, Lorenzo's patronage of humanists, such as Ficino, Poliziano, and Pico, his use of humanistically educated men in political and diplomatic posts, his creation of the Medici library, and his refounding of the University of Pisa contributed greatly to his renown as a wise ruler. Moreover, Lorenzo's literary training gave him the wherewithal to create an effective, sometimes eloquent style for his official letters and public speeches, and this was instrumental in many of his political successes. Both Machiavelli (979) and Guicciardini (3) comment on Lorenzo's skill in affecting and persuading his listeners, and if we can credit Machiavelli's account, when Lorenzo traveled alone to Naples and placed himself in the hands of his enemy, it was largely his eloquence and intellectual power that won over King Ferdinando and thereby saved Florence from a military disaster.

Not only Lorenzo's fame as a poet but also the motifs and symbols in his poems served at times to advance the Medici name. So, for example, the frequent punning connection that Lorenzo (Laurentius) makes between his name and the laurel tree (*lauro*), his personal device. The laurel is strategically invoked at the beginning of such poems as "The Supreme Good" (I.13), "The Partridge Hunt" (stanza 1), and "Ambra" (stanza 2), and its image recurs throughout the sonnets. Although the laurel here retains its usual Petrarchan and Apollonian associations, it also bears a distinctive political meaning. Cox-Rearick has observed that the evergreen laurel tree became a symbol of regeneration standing for the continuity and resilience of Medici rule. And as a symbol of the return of the Golden Age, it proclaimed the beneficence and pristine authority of Medicean government (15–20).

Even Lorenzo's decision to write his poems in Tuscan Italian rather than Latin had profound political implications, as he well knew. To write in Tuscan was to remind the world that the greatest Italian writers—Dante, Petrarch, and Boccaccio—were Tuscan. In the prologue to his "Commentary," where he justifies his use of the vernacular, Lorenzo pointedly calls them "our Florentine poets." To be sure, since the fourteenth century the vernacular had attracted few distinguished writers. Yet Lorenzo's decision to write in Tuscan helped spark a revival after a long spell of neglect, and this further enhanced the prestige of Florence's native tongue. Lorenzo also defended the use of the vernacular in the epistola to Federigo of Aragon, probably drafted by Poliziano in 1476. This letter serves as preface to the *Raccolta Aragonese*, the first known anthology of Italian poetry. Predictably, Lorenzo's selection gives pride of place to Dante and the Tuscan poets. The implication here is that the superiority of Tuscan both reflects and empowers Florence's privileged political role among the Italian states.

Lorenzo also favored the vernacular because, as he writes in "A Commentary," it was "well suited to move many people." He wanted to reach a large audience, not just the literati, and this goes a long way in explaining the broad appeal and popular subject matter of many of his poems. Only through the vernacular could Lorenzo incorporate in his writings the common speech of his ordinary citizens. And he did so freely, not only in the notorious carnival songs written for the festivals and in the farcical poems such as the "Symposium" and "The Partridge Hunt," but also in his more classical pieces, such as the "Corinto," where the shepherd uses common idioms of the Tuscan dialect. If we are to believe Renaissance accounts, Lorenzo possessed the common touch both in his life and in his art, and this helped him win the allegiance of common citizens, even as he proceeded to undermine the democratic institutions of Florence.

Many are the ways, then, in which Lorenzo's literary efforts may have served the interests of Medicean hegemony. Conversely, his political activities and the unusual range of worldly experience he gained through them lent his poems a realism and vitality unique to their age. Yet more often than not it is the tension between the claims of the *vita activa* and the *vita contemplativa* that finds expression in his writings, especially in his Neoplatonic poem "The Supreme Good," included in this anthology. It is a tension that can also be read in the features of his face as it is portrayed by Quattrocento artists.

The extant portraits of Lorenzo from his lifetime, now reproduced in Langedijk's monumental *Portraits of the Medici*, provide us with a vivid iconography of this divided self. The rugged face, framed by long straight hair usually cut just above shoulder length, sports a jutting jaw, a big, distinctive, twisted nose, firm thick lips, and large intelligent eyes. The Prague bust (see the frontispiece), which is probably by Antonio del Pollaiuolo, and the Washington bust, probably by Verrochio, are his most lifelike representations, and both display these features, which recur again and again in other contemporary portraits and in a large number of the posthumous paintings. It is not a refined or elegant face, but it is, like so much of his writing, vivid, earthy, and engaging. It is a face that projects the vigor and determination of a man of the world. But the high forehead, introspective gaze, and expression of concern or rumination that arises from the slightly knitted brow work to counteract this first impression: these features seem to divulge an unworldly tendency.

The portraits made in his lifetime also reveal, indirectly, a good deal about the artistic side of Lorenzo's personality. Most of them share a common style or approach in representing their subject. It seems reasonable to infer that Lorenzo encouraged, or at least permitted, this style. He was, after all, a connoisseur himself (Gombrich 54), and as the prologue to his "Commentary" (included here) shows, he was deeply concerned about how he might appear to the Florentine public. To some extent, then, we can view these portraits as self-portraits. Their manner, in fact, reflects significant aspects of Lorenzo's poetic style.

Lorenzo's contemporary portraits are rarely idealized. If anything, some of them seem to border on caricature. Few of them, for instance, tone down the rough, irregular features that are so pronounced in the death mask. In describing these portraits, Langedijk often refers to the face as ugly. Lorenzo, then, must have wanted to be depicted, and remembered, as he really looked, in all his homeliness. The verisimilitude of these likenesses, their frank rendering of the plain and homespun, the impression of roughness they give, are in fact all striking visual equivalents of the poetic realism found in Lorenzo's longer poems. The unadorned manner in which Lorenzo allowed himself to be portrayed became, in fact, an embarrassment to the late eighteenth and nineteenth centuries, when such "ugliness . . . did not seem to tally with the *virtù* of its subject" (Langedijk 1:32). It is no coincidence, I think, that Lorenzo's own style in poetry—candid, coarse, and sometimes rough and fragmentary—often raised the hackles of nineteenth-century critics.

In his portraits Lorenzo's irregular features almost seem to have been cut carelessly from stone and left unfinished. This suggestion of rough-hewn stone is a curious figuration of Lorenzo's keen interest in rocks and gems. Stone recurs so often as a leitmotif in his life that it begins to acquire an archetypal resonance, and when it does crop up, it usually has some-thing to tell us about the man.

If we accept Mary McCarthy's thesis in *The Stones of Florence*, the substance that best expresses Florence and the character of its people is stone. The city's geography is one of "towering rock and stone" (20), and the proverbial hardness and frugality of its inhabitants were probably formed by their environment. Also, Florentine art is characterized by its sculpturesque qualities (87). That great worker of stone, Michelangelo, was Florentine, and it was Lorenzo himself who discovered and encour-aged the young sculptor. It thus seems especially fitting that Lorenzo, who was regarded in his own and later periods as personifying Florence, should have been so fascinated by stone.

Lorenzo was an ardent, expert collector of precious stones and carved gems, especially ones from antiquity that represented mythological subjects (see Dacos). He also developed a fine collection of ancient vases cut from *pietra dura*, now on display in the Sala Buia of the Pitti palace. Because of his nearsightedness, these were among the few forms of visual art that he could enjoy fully. Nor is it extravagant to see a connection between his appreciation of gems and the keen attention to intricate, iridescent detail that distinguishes his poetic style.

His family *impresa* included a diamond ring, which is a motif in many of his portraits, and it was probably a gemstone ring that the blacksmith Bartolomeo Masi mentioned when he recorded in his diary the rumor that "a freak storm in April 1492 was caused by the release of a spirit that Lorenzo de' Medici, . . . lying gravely ill, had long kept imprisoned in a ring" (Gage 38). Whether Lorenzo actually believed, as did so many of his contemporaries, in the magical powers of precious stones is uncertain, but we do know that stones and rocks were a strong stimulus to his imag-ination. At one point he writes that "regarding certain kinds of stones, that are full of veins, there is often formed also therein that which pleases the *fantasia*" (quoted in Summers 122). Appropriately, the central episode of his finest poem, "Ambra," is the moving transformation of a wood nymph into rock.

Nearly all of these examples involve wonderful metamorphoses of stone, a symbol of matter in its extremity, into vivid spiritual or imaginal forms, or vice versa, as in the story of the nymph. In the carved gems, hard, intractable stone has been transformed into wondrously tiny mythological scenes. In "Ambra" a mythological being is changed into rock. In Lo-renzo's mind the chaotic veins of a stone form figures that satisfy the imagination. For Lorenzo, as for Michelangelo, the transformation of stone seems to have been an emblem of the imaginative, artistic process itself. Significantly, both artists were disposed to arrest, prematurely, the artistic process, leaving works unfinished, *non finiti*, thus calling attention to the process itself, to the dialectic of stone and sculpture, of raw language and poetic form.

Condivi's account of Lorenzo's discovery of Michelangelo, which is so rich in stone associations, shows Lorenzo in his element. At the same time it gives us a revealing picture of Lorenzo's personal style and artistic inclinations. The scene takes place two years before Lorenzo's death, in the Medici garden of San Marco, where Lorenzo had set up a number of ancient stone statues. Young Michelangelo, who often went there to study the statues, one day decided to copy the laughing, bearded head of a faun, whose mouth had been worn down beyond recognition. Michelangelo got a scrap of marble from the stone that Lorenzo was having cut there for his library:

> He set about copying the Faun with such care and study that in a few days he perfected it, supplying from his imagination all that was lacking in the ancient work, that is, the open mouth as of a man laughing, so that the hollow of the mouth and all the teeth could be seen. In the midst of this, the Magnificent Lorenzo, coming to see what point his works had reached, found the boy engaged in polishing the head and, approaching quite near, he was much amazed, considering first the excellence of the work and then the boy's age; and, although he did praise the work, nonetheless he joked with him as with a child and said, "Oh, you have made this Faun old and left him all his teeth. Don't you know that old men of that age are always missing a few?"
>
> To Michelangelo it seemed a thousand years before the Magnificent went away so that he could correct the mistake; and, when he was alone, he removed an upper tooth from his old man, drilling the gum as if it had come out with the root, and the following day he awaited the Magnificent with eager longing. When he had come and noted the boy's goodness and simplicity, he laughed at him very much; but then, when he weighed in his mind the perfection of the thing and the age of the boy, he who was the father of all *virtù*, resolved to help and encourage such great genius and to take him into his household. (12)

We first see Lorenzo, characteristically enough, coming to check up on the stone he was having cut. His jest, built on the image of the old toothless faun, echoes the humor we find in such poems as "The Partridge Hunt" and "Symposium," which are included in this anthology. The image of the old faun, which inspires the young stonecarver to remove one of the teeth, also reflects the same delight in concrete particulars that informs both Lorenzo's poems and his portraits. As we have seen, he was not one to gloss over the seamy side of existence. Condivi's anecdote neatly sums up many of Lorenzo's salient traits as man and as poet, among them his benevolence, his human understanding and artistic discernment, his earthy humor, and his love of worked stone.

II

Though renowned as a Renaissance ruler and patron, Lorenzo is hardly known at all in the English-speaking world as a major Quattrocento poet, whose literary works run to over five hundred pages.

The range of literary genres in which Lorenzo wrote is astonishingly wide. Besides the hundred sonnets, canzoni, and sestine in his canzoniere, Lorenzo wrote the following works in verse: a narrative about a falconry expedition ("The Partridge Hunt"), a satire on wine drinking that parodies the *Inferno* ("Symposium"), a Neoplatonic discourse on happiness ("The Supreme Good"), dance and carnival songs, such as "The Triumph of Bacchus and Ariadne," considered by many to be the finest lyrical poem of the Quattrocento, bawdy carnival songs, such as the "Song of the Village Lasses," a pastoral lament ("Corinto"), a humorous parody of a pastoral lament whose attribution to Lorenzo is controversial ("Nencia of Barberino"), an Ovidian romance about the attempted rape of a nymph by a river god ("Ambra"), and two *silvae*, the second of which is so replete with mythical figures and allegories that it reads like the program for a Botticelli painting ("Wood of Love"). Not included in this anthology are a religious play in verse about the era of Constantine and Julian the Apostate ("La rappresentazione di S. Giovanni e Paolo") and numerous devotional poems and hymns. In prose, he wrote a ribald story in the manner of Boccaccio ("The Novella of Giacoppo"), a literary treatise, which includes a defense of the vernacular and his own poetry ("A Commentary on My Sonnets"), and hundreds of letters.

A few of Lorenzo's lyrics regularly find their way into anthologies of Italian poetry in English, but otherwise very little of his literary oeuvre has been translated, the most important omission being his longer narrative and didactic poems. This omission alone constitutes one of the most undeserved cases of neglect in the history of Anglo-Italian literary relations. Since the publication of Sara Sturm's *Lorenzo de' Medici* (1974), we are in the embarrassing position of having a major American study of Lorenzo's literary writings while the writings themselves remain unavailable in English.

An English version of Lorenzo's literary works for readers who do not command Italian is thus long overdue. First of all, the literary works are important for understanding Lorenzo as a historical figure. Like his contemporaries Columbus and Leonardo da Vinci, Lorenzo is a source of fascination to a large body of readers, who would read his literary works for their documentary value. Because of his wide-ranging activities as banker, ruler, and patron, Lorenzo's writings are of significance to a much broader audience than that of the literary specialists. This is especially so since it has become axiomatic in Laurentian studies that "his poems are a major source for our understanding of Lorenzo" (Fryde 140).[2] They reveal, for example, the largely unknown private side of the public figure. In his humorous sketches of Florentine life we discover his fascination with the foibles of his fellow citizens, his predilection for slapstick comedy, and the enjoyment he got in the good-natured teasing of his friends. Almost everywhere we encounter Lorenzo's love of the outdoors, his delight in the beauty of the Tuscan countryside and in the many pleasures it offered, from falcon hunting and swimming to observing the habits of shepherds, foxes, and owls, and lying sprawled among the wildflowers in a favorite glade. We share his pride, and his weariness, in being Florence's leading

---

2. A number of recent historical and biographical works, some of them popular, make substantial use of Lorenzo's literary writings. See, for example, Hale 1977, Hook 1984, Hibbert 1985, and Cloulas 1986. Critical interest in Lorenzo's literary writings has grown steadily over the last three decades. In the wake of the ground-breaking biographical and literary studies of the 1960s, by Bigi, Rochon, Martelli, and Maier, the 1970s was a period of intense critical activity, with important studies by Tateo, Sturm, Orvieto, Zanato, and Hook, and with the inception of the systematic publication of Lorenzo's correspondence (1977–81). In the 1980s critical editions of many of Lorenzo's most important works have appeared, notably *La Nencia da Barberino* (1982), which is usually ascribed to Lorenzo, the *Canzoniere* (1984), the *Selve d'amore* under the title *Stanze* (1986), and the *Ambra* (1986). These studies and editions have provided both the critical justification and the textual basis for translating Lorenzo into English.

citizen. We get to know the distinctive character of his humanism when he refashions classical myth into a characteristically Tuscan shape. And we are alternately shocked and delighted at the wide range of his sensibility, which moves easily and quickly from popular slang to philosophical discourse, from ribaldry to Neoplatonic mysticism.

Second, the English-speaking public should have access to Lorenzo's literary works because these portray so vividly the times in which he lived. His is the major poetic voice of the Florentine Renaissance. In his longer poems, for example, he presents in a fresh and vital manner many of the central concerns, everyday activities, and favorite ideas of his day. As the nineteenth-century critic Symonds stated, Lorenzo "lived in close sympathy with his age, never rising above it, but accurately representing its main tendencies" (323). And Bigi (1961) concludes that Lorenzo's work "remains an extremely interesting record of Florentine culture and taste" (696). His longer poems, for example, are important sources for our understanding of Renaissance mythography.[3]

Finally, Lorenzo made original contributions to the poetry of his time. Through his defense of the vernacular (in "A Commentary"), through his patronage of Pulci and Poliziano, and through his decision to write his own poems in Italian, Lorenzo helped spark the revival of Italian poetry after a fallow period of seventy-five years. His writing in already established genres, such as the Dante parody ("Symposium"), the hunting poem ("The Partridge Hunt"), and the pastoral lament ("Corinto"), produced poems that are regarded by many as the best of their kind in his period. And with "Nencia of Barberino," if it is indeed his, he created a new subgenre of the pastoral ("versi nenciali"), which inspired numerous imitations throughout the fifteenth and sixteenth centuries (Tateo 8–9).

Another distinctive feature of Lorenzo the poet is his realism: it is that which sets him apart from his age, yet also makes him such a vivid portrayer of it.[4] From his early humorous verse to his later classicizing poems, Lorenzo's longer pieces are distinguished by a sharp focus on concrete particulars and by a shrewd understanding of psychological processes. Ear-

---

3. They are cited or analyzed in three seminal studies in this field. See Wind 41, 54–55, 59, 76–77; Levin 38–42; and Bush 74. More recently, two major studies of Renaissance art and aesthetics have benefited from a close reading of Lorenzo's literary writings. See Cox-Rearick 1984, 76–77, 84, and Summers 1981, 121–24, 242–45, 325, 345, 371–72. See also Burke, passim.

4. Concerning Lorenzo's realism, I am indebted here and in the next section to Maier's penetrating study, "Il realismo letterario di Lorenzo il Magnifico" (1969).

lier critics, such as De Sanctis, deplored Lorenzo's realism, his explicitness, and contrasted it invidiously to the *idealtà* of Poliziano (337). De Sanctis and some later critics seem vexed that Lorenzo dared to depart from an exquisiteness that they felt was quintessentially Quattrocento. In this light Lorenzo is seen as an intruder, as "a rude commoner [who] remained profoundly tied to this reality, to material things, as opposed to the ideas of the 'Ficinians'" (Garin 191).

That Lorenzo deviates from some of the poetic norms of his time is in fact a mark of his vitality and creativity. To neglect his verse because of its "untimely" realism is to falsify our picture of the Quattrocento. Lorenzo's style, with its poetic realism and its deft use of popular speech, reflects, after all, the *realpolitik* and mercantile sensibility of his Florence. It occupies an important middle ground between the refinement of Poliziano and the inspired farce of Pulci. From this perspective alone, the availability of his works in English will serve to modify and enlarge our usual conception of the Florentine Renaissance.

III

In his "Commentary," Lorenzo states that he wrote poetry out of a need for solace (*refrigerio*), for he had been much persecuted by men and fortune (Bigi 1965, 305). Poetry, then, was a pleasurable escape for him. Yet he also must have hoped that his fame as a poet would be lasting. Martelli has shown that Lorenzo corrected and added to his work throughout his life (1965, passim). Like Michelangelo, he was a compulsive reviser, and this squares with the notion that he had his eye on posterity.

If, however, Lorenzo thought that his poetry would be the source of his future fame, he was mistaken. In spite of the praise of Pico and Poliziano, in spite of Renaissance editions of his poems and treatise, his reputation as a poet lagged far behind his fame as a statesman. Sturm observes that if Lorenzo had not been so great a politician, his fame as a poet would have been much greater (7). Since he was such a powerful statesman, critics have always been tempted to dismiss his poetry as the pastime of a dilettante. This deeply rooted prejudice helps explain a fascinating curiosity of reception history: the fact that most of Lorenzo's major poems have never been translated into English.

But this has not been the only circumstance that has prevented him from having the audience he deserves. In the Victorian age, when Lorenzo should have found a translator, the bawdy, irreverent matter of many of his best poems assured that these would remain unenglished. Even in a century so little prim and proper as our own, it is curious that his more irreverent long poems, such as "Symposium" and "The Partridge Hunt," were not included in either the French or German translations of his work (see Chastel 1947 and Stange 1940). But a more important obstacle to his acceptance in the twentieth century has been a decisive shift in poetic taste away from longer poems that tell a story or that are didactic in character. Dominated by modernist poetics and Crocean aesthetics, the early twentieth century favored the lyric or the long poem composed of lyrical fragments. Symptomatic of this tendency is the reference to Lorenzo's poetry in a Pisan canto of Ezra Pound: "Lorenzo / who left lyrics inoltre / that men sing to this day" (canto 78). Lorenzo the poet, when known at all, is known for his lyrics, which are much less important than his longer poems.

The sheer difficulty of translating Lorenzo's longer poems also played a part in keeping translators away. Roscoe in the eighteenth century and Fryde and Angeleri in our own have agreed on how formidable this challenge is. Roscoe refused to try to translate the humorous poems (434), and Fryde laments that "Lorenzo's great skill in using with subtlety and delicacy the Tuscan language of his day" made translation problematic (140n). The particular flavor of Lorenzo's humor, dependent as it often is on colorful dialect expressions, is especially hard to carry over into another language. Exacerbating this problem have been uncertainties about Lorenzo's text and his meaning, and the lack, until recently, of sound critical editions of the longer poems. In addition to these factors, there arose in the early nineteenth century more specific moral, political, and aesthetic objections to Lorenzo's poetry that remained influential into the early part of our century.

Lorenzo's broad humor and his keen satirical sense often offended the more delicate taste of later periods. His reputation as a philanderer and the sexual candor of his carnival songs combined to excite the moral outrage of Victorians in particular. Symonds, for example, condemns the carnival songs as "uniformly and deliberately immoral" (339), and he complains of the "gross innuendos" and the "careless self-abandonment to carnal impulse" (338) in the dance songs. An early twentieth-century edition of these songs bears the title *Canzoni scandalose* (1927). And even André Chastel, who in 1947 published them in French, speaks of their "intolerable vulgarity" (8). These works, his most exuberantly bawdy, seem rather tame by late twentieth-century standards. The allegorization of sexual matters in terms of various Renaissance trades is ingenious but also somewhat mechanical. I have included one carnival song of this type: "Song of the Village Lasses."

The role played by bigotry in the misreading of Lorenzo's work is amusingly illustrated by the reception history of Lorenzo's brilliant satire on wine-drinking and gluttony, "Symposium." Already in 1763, the Bergamo edition had left out the eighth capitolo because it was "deficient and licentious" (Roscoe 432), an omission I have repaired in this translation. Symonds, in 1881, complained of the "brutality" of the poem's humor, and, not unambiguously, compared its realism to that of Dutch tavern pictures, which share with it "the same intellectual enjoyment of sensuality, the same animalism studied by an acute aesthetic spirit" (334). Though Roscoe in the eighteenth century recognized the poem for what it was, "a lively and severe reprehension of drunkenness" (155), the twentieth-century German critic Stange completely misinterpreted it, reading it as a *carpe diem* paean to drunkenness (xxvi). Others thought the poem to be sacrilegious, for Lorenzo freely drew on the themes, stylistic devices, and narrative strategies of the *Divine Comedy*, a text sacred to nineteenth-century literati. Symonds calls the parody of Dante "loathsome" (334n), and Castaldo, following Carducci, finds it "indecent" (*sconveniente*) (16). The satire is in fact no more indecent or scatological than the treatment of flattery or barratry in the *Inferno*. In yet another example, cited by Sturm (45), the Victorian critic Horsburgh found one particular passage in the "Symposium" to include the "most revolting conceit in literature." The reader must take his word for it, because he refuses to translate the passage, which ridicules the drunkenness and hypocrisy of a clergyman:

> The third one—whom you see already—studies,
>   once in a while, theology: he's earned
>   a doctorate—from his drinking buddies;   81
> and he has comprehended that the worst
>   chastisement suffered by our Lord on earth
>   was when he cried out from the cross, "I thirst."   84
>   (capitolo 4)

Horsburgh waxes so indignant that he misses Lorenzo's irony and utterly fails to distinguish Lorenzo's voice from the voice of characters whose ideas or conduct he derides.

Another sort of objection to Lorenzo's poetry was political. Nineteenth-century historians and critics who, like Sismondi and De Sanctis, defended liberal democratic values saw Lorenzo's policies as undermining the republican liberties of Florence. Lorenzo did in fact manipulate the city's governing bodies to increase his own power at the expense of local democracy. In the eighteenth century Roscoe could see in Lorenzo a forerunner of the enlightened despot, but Sismondi viewed him as a tyrant.

One consequence of the political critique of Lorenzo was that critics were less likely to take Lorenzo's poetry seriously as poetry. When his art was not ignored or rejected on ad hominem grounds, it was viewed essentially as an instrument of political domination (Maier 1969, 2) or as a means of corrupting the political will of the people (Palmarocchi 12). Symonds echoes this *panem et circenses* interpretation when he writes that "the serious purpose which underlay Lorenzo's cultivation of popular poetry was to amuse the crowd with pageantry and music, to distract their attention from state concerns and to blunt their political interest" (336). He is thinking particularly of Lorenzo's carnival and dance songs. Even Lorenzo's Neoplatonic poetry was seen as having a political agenda: to encourage the *vita contemplativa* was also to discourage the virtues of political participation. As Maier has shown, such arguments have been popular with scholars, for they offer a reassuring way of accounting for the disconcerting fact that Lorenzo was both politico and poet (1969, 2).

It is again Maier who has raised some serious doubts about the early political interpretation of Lorenzo's poetry: there is very little overt political content in his poems, and Lorenzo obviously took a genuine delight in letters for their own sake. Rather, poetry was for him a means of escaping the political realm (1969, 3, 12–13). But as I have already shown, none of this is proof that his poems did not also serve, in a subtle way, Medicean politics. Indeed, the last decade, inspired by a new historicism, has witnessed a revival of the political interpretation of Lorenzo's cultural activities, including his poetry writing. These new interpretations, though at times reductionist, are not as dismissive as the earlier ones, and they have thrown a good deal of light on the functions of Laurentian symbolism in its historical context.[5]

5. See the studies by Zanato, Elam, Cox-Rearick, Jordan, Gombrich, Langedijk, and Bullard.

IV

The traditional aesthetic critique of Lorenzo's poetry rests on claims that his style is insufficiently polished and that certain poems seem fragmentary. Criticism of the unfinished quality of Lorenzo's longer poems has also had a depressing effect on his standing as a poet, especially among mainstream Italian critics, who continue to set a great value on an elegant, polished style, euphoniousness, and a high degree of aesthetic closure. In this regard it seems singularly appropriate that the only monument marking Lorenzo's mortal remains is Michelangelo's unfinished statue of a Madonna and Child. This sculpture is one of Michelangelo's great *non finiti*, and thus a fitting reminder that, as with Michelangelo's sculptures, so with Lorenzo's poems: no convincing interpretation of them can avoid coming to terms with their "unfinished" status and the aesthetic significance of this.

One mode of the Laurentian *non finito* occurs in those of his works that break off before they have been concluded. Two of Lorenzo's major works fall in this category: the "Symposium," which breaks off in the middle of capitolo 8 (in Martelli's critical edition), and "A Commentary."[6] This mode of the *non finito* is not very extensive in Lorenzo, nor does there seem to have been an aesthetic purpose in leaving these works unconcluded. That is, the lack of an ending does not seem to contribute to the artistic quality or power of the works in question.

A more significant mode of the *non finito* in Lorenzo, found in many of his longer poems, manifests itself as a certain roughness of poetic texture or structure, where, for instance, diction and detail seem insufficiently "poetic," or where the integration of the poem's parts seems defective, giving the impression that they have been juxtaposed rather than mortised together. Critics have variously described Lorenzo's style as careless, overly colloquial, or too full of realistic detail. Thus Roscoe remarks on the "rusticity" of Lorenzo's language (147), and De Sanctis, writing on the "Selve d'amore," claims that the defect of Lorenzo's poetry is "precisely its immoderate naturalism" which serves "a minutely-depicted reality, observed and reproduced exactly in its external characteristics, and not idealized or rendered with a delicate and fluid artistry" (337). Concerning the same poem, Bigi notes the imperfect integration of its parts (1961, 703).

---

6. Several of Lorenzo's minor works, such as "Apollo and Pan" and the novella of Ginevra, are incomplete in this way.

Some of these traditional criticisms recur in Bessi's introduction to her important critical edition of the "Ambra" (1986). Appropriately, the title of the introduction is "Un opera aperta?"[7] Bessi documents Lorenzo's "predilection for fragmented and fragmentable structures," which she finds in the disconnectedness of his images and in the fact that details are not always subordinated to the general framework (14, 10). She remarks on a certain "intemperance" in the descriptions, especially in the amplification of seemingly irrelevant particulars (11). Finally, in an arresting image that she takes from Lorenzo's Ovidian poem "Ambra," Bessi compares Lorenzo's poetry to the limbs of the wood nymph Ambra, which, as she is turned into rock, resemble "a figure sketched, / but left unfinished (non finita), in the solid stone" (20, "Ambra," stanza 41).

Bessi's use of Lorenzo's sculpturesque simile suggests that the best approach to Lorenzo's poetics is not by way of Poliziano but rather through the *non finiti* of Michelangelo. As in Lorenzo's poems, so in Michelangelo's sculptures, many of the figures remain rough, "sketched but left unfinished in the solid stone." In the *Battle of the Centaurs and Lapiths*, for example, the background is roughed out and not polished, and the hair of the figures resembles unworked rough stone more than it does hair. In the *Madonna of the Stairs* the two background figures are conspicuously rough and incomplete, their unfinished feet oddly contrasting to the polished steps on which they rest. Each of these works was executed in Lorenzo's lifetime, so he may well have known them. Most of Michelangelo's later works, ranging from the Pitti tondo to the Duomo *Pietà*, are also *non finiti*, and how to interpret them remains a central issue in Michelangelo studies.

Many of the explanations given for Michelangelo's *non finiti* could apply to Lorenzo's as well. For Michelangelo, as for Lorenzo, it has been argued that the artist simply had insufficient time to put the finishing touches on the work at hand. From Vossler (74) to the present day, critics have hinted that Lorenzo's busy life kept him from polishing his works. Another explanation is that each artist was a compulsive reviser, that neither could leave off altering, changing, adding, or subtracting (Schulz, pas-

---

7. Bessi does not really answer the intriguing question posed in the title of her introduction. That is, she does not attempt to account for the open, fragmentary structure of the "Ambra" by using the critical framework developed by Umberto Eco in "L'opera aperta." Yet her analysis, much more than her critical evaluation, of the poem provides valuable evidence for treating this work as a *non finito*, in other words, as an early modern manifestation of the *opera aperta*. See Eco 1–23.

sim). In the case of sculpture, amplification is less of an issue, but the research of Martelli suggests that Lorenzo continually revised his work, adding new sections that were imperfectly integrated and polished (1965). Never satisfied with a work, he could rarely bring it to a finished state.

Another explanation, which might also apply to Lorenzo, is that Michelangelo intentionally left his works unfinished because he thought of the rough areas as serving an artistic function in the context of the whole work. Thus Tolnay suggests that the *non finiti* may have resulted from "artistic necessity" (95). He presents us with the following idea: although Michelangelo must have known full well that his works were unfinished, "he did not complete his statues, in spite of this, because in so doing he would have lessened their lyric intensity" (95). Hibbard speculates that Michelangelo may have become enamored with "the mere process of revealing, of gradually uncovering his figures, and he may slowly have begun to feel the attraction of the potential and unrealized—of Becoming as opposed to Being" (174–75). Such an attraction is, as we shall see, palpable in Lorenzo's great poem "Ambra." Although intentionality is difficult to prove, it is worth noting that Vasari, in sculpture, and Poliziano, in poetry, defended the artistic validity of the *non finito* (Summers 226, 476, 523). So there may well have been a climate of opinion that encouraged the deliberate creation of *non finiti*.

Even if we remain skeptical of the conscious, or for that matter unconscious, intentionality of the *non finiti*, we can still discuss how they affect us. There does seem to be a fairly wide agreement among moderns that Michelangelo's *non finiti* are wonderfully effective. Whatever Michelangelo's intent may have been, the incompleteness of the Boboli slaves, for instance, creates an effect of particular force and integrity: they are art, but at the same time they declare their bondage to the stone from which they have been incompletely liberated. If, as Michelangelo said, sculpture is the "art that takes away superfluous material," then the *non finiti*, by leaving some superfluous stone, call attention to the medium itself and to the process of its transformation. In this sense a *non finito* behaves like an *òpera aperta*.

In many of Lorenzo's longer poems similar effects are to be found. There are stanzas that display the burnish of the lapidary cut, but then there are those in which the poetic material is less worked, where the surface is marked by the rough cut. In stanza 18 of the "Ambra," for instance, the simile, which compares the roar of the torrent to an earthquake, does not seem to be smoothly worked into the text (Bessi 1986,

14). It sticks out, a bit awkwardly. It is like a stony protuberance in a sculpture in which too much superfluous material has been left. Yet the effect is not without its artistry. The ungainly insertion of stanza 18 reflects, on a formal level, the disregard for limits and "good form" of the wild, swollen torrent that is being described and compared to the earthquake.

Likewise, as Bessi observes, other sections of the "Ambra" betray a "descriptive superfluity of detail" (10). Part I of the poem is a description of the Tuscan winter. But in stanzas 9 and 10, the image of the migratory cranes, which is appropriate to the constellation of winter images, suddenly expands to include a description of the flock in its warm tropical quarters, where it is threatened by an eagle:

> And often will the eagle slowly glide
> Above the water, menacing the throng:
> The cranes rise up as one and drive it hence
> Before a blast of loudly beating wings,
> But should one crane forsake the feathered flock,
> The agile eagle quickly swoops it up:
> The victim is deceived if it believes
> That it is borne to Jove like Ganymede.
>
> (stanza 10)

With its introduction of particulars not pertinent to winter, this stanza illustrates what Bessi calls Lorenzo's "descriptive intemperance" (11). Yet the vivid detail and wit of this superfluous material quickly overcomes whatever unease we feel over the violation of classical economy. Moreover, the figure of the Jovian eagle, with its blend of nature and divinity, with its allusion to rape, adumbrates the story of the river god Ombrone and the wood nymph Ambra in part II. And it is in fact a warm day when Ambra first takes a dip in the Ombrone, thus awaking the river's lust (stanza 24).

Similar to the paratactic order at the stanza level is the tenuous articulation of parts I and II of "Ambra," that is, of the description of winter and the story of Ombrone and Ambra. The imperfect integration of these two parts, or fragments, has often been remarked (cf. Bessi 27–29). Juxtaposed rather than thoroughly meshed together, the two parts are nevertheless related, the burden of integration resting on a subtle web of thematic resonances concerning rivers, violence, and the myriad forms of transformation. The lack of explicit articulation between the parts creates a wonderful effect of suggestiveness not unlike that provoked by Michelangelo's *non finiti*.

It is significant that the *non finito* is itself a motif of the poem "Ambra," not simply one of its constitutive principles. As we have seen, the unfinished work of sculpture is a key image used to evoke the metamorphosis of the nymph Ambra into a rock.

The image occurs in the climax of part II, which is an Ovidian tale of attempted rape and metamorphosis. The wood nymph Ambra, pursued over the Tuscan countryside by the river Ombrone, who is also a god, is saved in the nick of time by being turned into a rock. In the narrative Lorenzo, with great effect, dwells on that moment in the process of petrification in which Ambra still shows some of her womanly form and has not yet become amorphous rock. The imagery of transformation that pervades the whole poem here reaches its climax. Ambra, in desperation, has just cried out to Diana to save her from the river:

> These words had hardly issued from her mouth
> When both of her white feet were seized by an
> Unusual rigidity. You see
> Them grow and turn to stone. You see the color
> Of legs and lovely torso change, and yet
> You would believe this was a woman still:
> Her limbs look like a human figure sketched,
> But left unfinished, in the solid stone.
>
> (stanza 41)

The pathos of metamorphosis is intensified by the suggestive image of the *non finito*.

Here Lorenzo betrays a fascination with the borderline state between inchoate and complete representation. He implies that the recognition of the figure roughed out in the material is even more intense because the figure is incomplete (cf. stanza 44.1–4). That Lorenzo must have been critically aware of this perceptual puzzle is shown in a passage from his "Commentary," where he writes that there are "sometimes in the clouds of the air diverse and strange forms of animals and men; and, regarding certain kinds of stones, that are full of veins, there is often formed also therein that which pleases the *fantasia*" (quoted in Summers 122). Thus intermediate states between formlessness and completion, such as those found in *non finiti*, can be powerful sources of pleasure to the imagination. The combined force of these two passages leads to the conclusion that Lorenzo too was conscious of the aesthetic effects he was creating when he left certain sections of his work in a rough or fragmentary state. Like so many of Lorenzo's other major poems, "Ambra" enacts in its own formation a dialectic of form and substance, which for Lorenzo, as for Michelangelo, is the powerful expression of a new aesthetics.[8]

Lorenzo's ability to write well in a disconcertingly wide range of genres has sometimes been held against him. His poetic oeuvre encompasses a Neoplatonic poem, devotional poems, bawdy carnival songs, sonnets, a hunting poem, a satirical parody of Dante, mythological poems, pastoral poems, an Ovidian tale, two *silvae*, and a *sacra rappresentazione*. Earlier critics wondered how any one poet could cover so much territory. One solution to this puzzle was to say that Lorenzo did not really care about the content of his poems (Maier 1954, 265), that their wide range reflected his dilettantism, superficiality, and overall lack of seriousness (Orvieto 1976, 93). Finally, the diversity of his poetic personae seemed to call into question his personal "sincerity."

Such views have all but disappeared in the second half of the twentieth century. Research on the chronology of Lorenzo's literary works has revealed a coherent pattern of development: his humorous, satirical works come earlier, followed by a Neoplatonic phase, and at the end of his life appear his more classical, mythological works (Bigi 1961, 697; Maier 1969, 9–10). In this context Lorenzo's eclecticism is less bewildering, and charges of insincerity lose their force. Others have argued that his multiplicity is "modern," and that the intensity of his approach sets him apart from dilettantism (Orvieto 1976, 96, 98). Moreover, Maier sees Lorenzo's eclecticism as an expression of his role as poet-reader and poet-translator, which allowed him to assimilate, vernacularize, and develop inherited poetic forms (Maier 1969, 6, 11). Today, Lorenzo's delight in experimenting with a diversity of generic codes will strike many as being a postmodern quality.

From these new perspectives Lorenzo's derivativeness no longer seems such a stigma. All texts, we now know, are intertextual. As Maier says, Lorenzo especially enjoyed "composing his own music out of a pre-existing music" (Maier 1969, 8). It was not only his work as a defender of the

---

8. For the intriguing possibility that Lorenzo may have had a decisive influence on Michelangelo's aesthetics, see Gombrich 57 and Summers 180.

vernacular but also as a poet-translator that earned Lorenzo the reputation of being the renewer of Italian literature (Roscoe 133). He enriched immeasurably the vernacular literature of this time by introducing into it a wide array of topoi, themes, and myths of classical origin. He was also the first to offer an Italian form of the Latin *silva*.

Yet the importance of Lorenzo's role as poet-translator should not obscure for us his innovations and his singular place in Quattrocento letters. He developed the carnival song of his time in a new direction and, if he is indeed the author of "Nencia," introduced a new genre with that poem. As Bigi has noted, even when Lorenzo's works are most indebted to others, his poetic style is his own (1961, 697). His treatment, for instance, of classical myth is different from that of his ancient sources and of his contemporaries. He succeeds in endowing myth with an unprecedented feeling of weight and reality (Maier 1969, 36). A pervasive feature of his poetic style is its realism. It is that which sets him most apart from his contemporaries. Whether it is giving the substance of the everyday to myth, or evoking nature in all its intricate detail, or describing human life in its earthy particulars, or using the language of peasants, or demystifying literary views of the pastoral life, or revealing a keen psychological penetration, or expressing subtle disenchantment with existence itself, Lorenzo's longer poems frequently present us with the illusion that we are experiencing the fresh, sharp, surprising taste of reality itself.

V
On the Texts and Translations

The size and variable quality of Lorenzo's literary opus have called for a process of careful sifting and selection, so while this anthology does not come close to including all of his works, it does embrace those that are, in my judgment, his best. Since a marked feature of his opus is its great variety of subject matter, genre, and mode, I have also tried to represent the diversity of Lorenzo's poetic personae and voices. Yet it will be clear that this selection gives more space to poetry than prose, and within his poetic opus, the emphasis is on his longer poems. The latter are not as well known as they should be, even among Renaissance specialists, and recent criticism has shown that Lorenzo's real literary achievement is in these longer pieces rather than in his lyric poetry.

With the longer poems I have as a rule included the whole work. Notable exceptions are the "Symposium," which is very episodic and incomplete in the original, and the second "Wood of Love," which I have not been able to translate in its entirety, though I do offer the major set pieces ("The Golden Age," etc.). The translation of "Nencia of Barberino" (the Volpi version) I have put in an appendix, in acknowledgment of the fact that its attribution to Lorenzo is still controversial (see Bessi 1982).

Not included are the first "Wood of Love," the religious play, and the poetic fragments "Apollo and Pan" and the "Furtum Veneris et Martis." No more than a few of Lorenzo's multitudinous sonnets have slipped in, and those, with the exception of the unrhymed version of "Oh shining star . . ." in "A Commentary," have been translated by other hands than my own. Nor have I included any of the religious capitoli or laudi, for I feel that the last capitolo of "The Supreme Good," based on a letter by Ficino, is a much more successful example of Lorenzo's religious poetry. Of the numerous carnival and dance songs only a handful of the more notable or representative specimens will be found. These, though, are perhaps Lorenzo's finest short poems.

From Lorenzo's voluminous prose writings (cf. the *Lettere*, 4 vols. to date), I have included a small selection. The comic novella and the prologue and first exposition of his "Commentary" offer interesting counterpoints to Lorenzo's poetry, while the selection of letters should give the reader a fuller sense of Lorenzo the man.

The order of arrangement is approximately chronological. It is approximate, first of all, because the dating of many of Lorenzo's works is still somewhat conjectural, and, second, because the items under the rubrics "Carnival and Dance Songs" and "Letters" cover different periods of the author's life.

Although Lorenzo's literary works have been published again and again from the fifteenth century to our own, no comprehensive, authoritative edition of these texts exists.[9] Instead, we have a collection of texts whose authority varies considerably. Fortunately, the valuable textual work of Martelli (1966 and 1965b), Chiari, and Bigi (1965) has been followed in the 1980s by a major effort to establish many more of Lorenzo's texts.

---

9. For a bibliography of the printed editions of Lorenzo's works, see Simioni 2:343–52. For some modern general editions, see the first entry in the Bibliography under Lorenzo de' Medici. The major early textual work was done by Simioni in 1913 and 1939, though much of this has been superseded. Bigi's anthology (1965) is not really a critical edition, but his textual choices and emendations are very useful.

Thus we now have reliable editions of the "Ambra" (Bessi 1986), the "Selve d'amore" (Castagnola, under the title "Stanze"), the "Canzoniere" (Orvieto 1984), and the several versions of "La Nencia da Barberino" (Bessi 1982). And in prose there is the ongoing publication of his *Lettere* (ed. Rubinstein and Fubini) and Zanato's forthcoming critical edition of the "Comento."

These editions have helped me greatly in interpreting Lorenzo's meaning. Though his meaning is not always difficult, there are plenty of cruxes and obscure passages, some due to textual corruption, others to grammatical ambiguities or the irretrievable meanings of particular archaic words or expressions. One wishes that Lorenzo had made commentaries for all his works. He himself was an unashamed adherent of the intentional fallacy, and he argued in his "Commentary" that for no one was the task of interpretation more appropriate "than for the author himself, because no one else is better able to know or truly determine what he means, as is shown clearly enough by the confusion that arises from the variety of commentaries, in which the commentators usually follow their own inclination rather than the true intention of the author" (Bigi 1965, 298). Every translation is also an interpretation, and so I hope that in these difficult passages my inclination has matched the author's intention.

A greater challenge than deciphering Lorenzo's meaning, though, has been finding in English the appropriate verse form, style, and tone to match each of Lorenzo's poems. The attempt to capture the flavor, nuances, and spirit of his diverse styles has been at once exhilarating and arduous. As Fryde has said, "Lorenzo's great skill in using . . . the Tuscan language of his day makes it particularly difficult to translate his poetry into any other language" (140; cf. Angeleri, passim).

For Lorenzo's early, humorous poems I use rhymed verse and for his later, more serious ones, blank verse. Rhyme, I feel, helps bring across Lorenzo's wit and humor in ways that unrhymed verse cannot: it provides a tunefulness and tautness that conveys well the esprit of these earlier texts. Rhyme in translation is sometimes attacked because it can result in inexact renderings and in a kind of forced syntax and diction that is alien to the modern ear. But by using simplified versions of the original rhyme schemes I have tried to avoid these problems. In the "Symposium," for example, I adopt a simplified terza rima (*a x a, b x b*, etc.), which permits some of the humorous effects of rhyme but does not interfere, as authentic terza rima would, with a reasonable standard of accuracy and a colloquial-sounding syntax. For most of the later poems—"Corinto" and the carnival and dance songs are exceptions—I have found unrhymed iambic pentameter more appropriate, partly because these works are so indebted to unrhymed Latin models.

The main difficulty I have had with Lorenzo's early long poems has been in conveying the rustic feel of Tuscan dialect and the humor generated by rhyme, alliteration, and special locutions. One of the most celebrated stanzas of "La Nencia," describing how Nencia herself dances, is a case in point:

> Ell'è dirittamente ballerina,
> ch'ella se lancia com'una capretta,
> girasi come ruota de mulina,
> e dassi della mano nella scarpetta;
> Quand'ella compie el ballo, ella se 'nchina,
> po' se rivolge e duo colpi iscambietta,
> e fa le più leggiadre riverenze
> che gnuna cittadina da Firenze.

The diminutive suffixes (from baller*ina* to cittad*ina* and through the *etta* rhymes) humorously convey a tone of affectionate condescension. The syntax is straightforward, and a colloquial flavor is imparted by the parataxis of the shepherd's speech. The rustic similes are funny, as is the final touch in the use of the Tuscan dialect word "gnuna" (i.e., "nessuna"). My English version tries to retain some of these effects:

> She is indeed a ballerina, and like
> A little goat she makes a leap or bound.
> She whirls about just like a waterwheel
> And slaps her little shoe that's left the ground.
> And when she ends the dance she bows, then makes
> Two little capers, once she's turned around:
> She curtsies much more prettily, one warrants,
> Than any woman living now in Florence.

Here, all the "littles" do not make up for the force of the diminutive suffixes in the original, but the parataxis and the similes come across in English. To make up for some of the losses, I add the alliteration on *w* in line 3, and I retain "ballerina" for its diminutive and for its humorously inappropriate preciousness in this context ("little dancer" would probably have been closer to the speaker's meaning). I also translate "colpi iscambietta" literally as "capers" to create a wordplay on "little goat." Though I lose both "cittadina" and "gnuna" in the last line, the feminine rhyme "warrants/Florence" works well: it is mildly amusing because of its unexpectedness.

By such compromises and displacements I have tried to maintain a higher level of poetic quality than would otherwise be possible. I have also tried to maintain a reasonable standard of accuracy and at the same time give the English-speaking reader a sense of the vitality, colloquial flavor, and humor of the originals. Translation of Lorenzo's later, classicizing poems such as the "Ambra" and "A Wood of Love" has entailed a different set of problems: the presentation of complex, extended similes; the sustaining of a more elevated style without sounding pompous; the retention of poetic intensity with the use of blank verse.

For the shorter poems—the dance and carnival songs—the simplified rhyme schemes have seemed to work well, and translating the last three of these has been a real pleasure. My attempted translations of Lorenzo's sonnets, on the other hand, have invariably failed to combine his rhyme scheme with an accurate rendering of the sense. Nor with this verse form did it seem fair to simplify the rhyme. As a result I have resorted to translations by others. Lorenzo himself claims in his "Commentary" that the sonnet is superior to other verse forms because of its difficulty: it is a form in which every word is crucial and in which it is difficult to avoid harshness of sound and obscurity of meaning. In my futile efforts to translate Lorenzo's sonnets, I have experienced the truth of these claims. Even so, the versions by other poets included here do deliver, I feel, something of the spirit of Lorenzo's better sonnets.

For Lorenzo's novella and his letters, I have also been able to find good translations by other hands. Neither the anonymous translation of the novella of Giacoppo nor Janet Ross's versions of the letters has required much revision.

Lorenzo's "Commentary on My Sonnets" already existed in two English versions, the first an incomplete, somewhat condensed paraphrase incorporated in Lipari's study of the "Commentary" (1st ed. 1936), and the second a rare, privately printed translation of the whole "Comento," published by Murray Linwood Marshall in 1949.[10] There are a number of

---

10. I am deeply indebted to Mr. Marshall's widow, Mrs. Hazel S. Seebode, for giving me a copy of this translation and for granting me permission to use it in this anthology.

inaccuracies in Marshall's version: these are due not only to the complexity of Lorenzo's prose but also to the fact that the translator worked without the benefit of later scholarship. Nor did he evidently know Lipari's admirable study. Nevertheless, Marshall's translation manages to convey very well the style of Lorenzo's prose: it has the right sentence rhythm, syntax, and stateliness. Consequently, I have used this version, but I have revised it extensively, and, where necessary, I have retranslated sentences and entire sections.

Besides being one of the most important contributions to Quattrocento literary criticism (Zanato 11–44), the prologue of Lorenzo's "Commentary" is a heady mixture of scholastic argumentation, Ficinian Neoplatonism and stil novistic rhetoric. Marshall's version and my revision endeavor to retain those elements of Lorenzo's style that are characteristic of his age but alien to ours. The version offered resists the temptation to modernize his prose, to do away with the prolixity, the emphatic hypotaxis, and the repetitiousness of his style. The sinews and sinuosities of Lorenzo's sentences have largely been left intact. The result may seem a bit strange, but it has the virtue of preserving, in the form of Lorenzo's language, a way of thinking that has all but disappeared.

SELECTED POEMS AND PROSE

The Partridge Hunt

1. By now the east had turned completely red.
   The mountain peaks seemed fashioned out of gold.
   The peasant was returning to his work—
   You heard the fledgling sparrow squawk and scold.
   The stars had fled, and you could almost see
   The one who loved the laurel tree of old.
   The horned owl, barn owl, and the night owl too,
   In quite a hurry to the woods withdrew.

2. The wolf retreated to its wilderness.
   The fox as well retreated to its den,
   For there was now a chance it might be seen,
   Now that the moon had come and gone again.
   The busy peasant woman had already
   Allowed the sheep and pigs to leave their pens.
   Crystalline, clear, and chilly was the air:
   The morning pledged the weather would be fair,

3. When I was roused by jingling bells and by
   The calling of the dogs and similar sounds.
   "Get up, let's go, make haste, you falconers.
   It's late. They're far away, our hunting grounds.
   The master of the dogs, let him go first
   To guarantee this morning that some hounds
   Do not get trampled on before the hunt.
   Please, Cappellaio, quickly to the front!"

4. So Cappellaio takes the lead and calls
   His dogs: Tamburo, Pezuol, Martello,

And Foglia and Castagna and Guerrina,
Rocca, Fagiano, Fagianin, Cappello,
Frizza, Bamboccio, Biondo, and Rosina;
Ghiotto, Corta, Viola, and Pestello,
My old Buontempo, Fuso, and Zambraccio,
Pennecchio, Serchio, Buratel, and Staccio.

5.   Now that the dogs have taken to the field
     Four riders with four sparrowhawks appear:
     Guglielmo—he who's always liked this sport,
     For whom it's been a habit many a year—
     Giovan Francesco, and behind him Foglia,
     Then Dionigi bringing up the rear—
     But early as it was, he was disposed
     To slump a bit, and as he rode, he dozed.

6.   But Fortune, she who always finds it fun
     To smear the one who's lily-white with muck,
     Makes Dionigi tumble from his horse,
     And on his left-hand side. That was bad luck,
     For falling so, he broke his hawk's right wing
     And crushed it badly on the side he struck.
     And strange to say, this pleased him well enough,
     For now he would not have to huff and puff.

7.   Not only did he fall, he kept on rolling,
     Believe me, till he rolled the whole way down,
     For hardly had he hit the slope than presto,
     He hit the bottom like a stone that's round.
     "To've stayed in bed this morning like Gismondo,"
     He then reflected, "would have been more sound:
     Unbooted, cool, in nothing but a shirt.
     I won't trip up again, if I escape unhurt.

8.   "Indeed I showed but very little sense
     When I went out at such an early hour.
     If I had stayed in bed, the hunters' plight,
     And mine as well, would not have been so sour.
     I'd have arranged a pleasant lunch and spread

A cloth adorned with many a pretty flower.
To crush one's bed and pillow has more charm
Than to crush horse and hawk, and come to harm."

9. Meanwhile he wants the hawk to take his fist,
But it's so badly hurt it can't achieve
Its perch, and even with its master's help
It falls again. From this he can perceive
That he will have to get another hawk.
And while he readjusts his open sleeve,
It claws his hand. He drives the hawk below,
Then jumps on it, and turns it into dough.

10. "Where is Corona? And Giovan Simone,
The one who has the great big nose, where's he?"
I asked. "There is a different reason for
Each one not coming," Braccio answered me.
"Corona's never caught a partridge yet,
Except by chance or accidentally.
If left behind, he will not take offense:
With him along, bad luck's the consequence.

11. "Giovan Simone's gone his merry way
Not having bid a single soul adieu.
He's gone into an inn, without permission,
So much he longs to give his thirst its due.
He always makes the dogs and horses skittish
Each time he puts his lordly nose askew:
Whoever sees him fears and runs away,
So each is glad Giovanni does not stay."

12. "And where is Pulci, that he can't be heard?"
"A while ago he went into that spread
Of trees, perhaps he wants to spin a sonnet—
He's sure to have some notion in his head.
Watch out, Corona, Pulci has some plan.
This morning he was muttering in his bed.
I heard him say your name: if I'm not wrong,
He'll skewer you in some lampoon or song."

13. So three continue on the partridge hunt,
     And lots of people come behind these three
     For fun or just to watch: Bartolo, Braccio,
     Ulivier, and then Parente, he
     Who'd never seen more gamebirds on the wing.
     I too set out among this company,
     With Alamann and Portinar, that one
     Who's like a barn owl in the noonday sun.

14. Behind all these, a bit apart, comes Strozzo,
     Who is the master of this retinue.
     Indeed, he seems to be a true adept
     For whom this sport can offer nothing new.
     At last we'd ridden through so many woods
     We reached the loveliest site that hitherto
     A living soul had ever seen: a place
     That nature made expressly for the chase.

15. One saw a perfect little vale, the sides
     Of which were clean and open like a glade,
     And then a little gulch with clumps of trees,
     And only there could one enjoy some shade.
     On every side there was a gentle slope
     Whose beauty, even to the blind, conveyed
     A longing for the hunt: all did admit,
     The world had never seen the likes of it.

16. Up on the ridge the sun already warms
     Their backs, while shade still fills the lower vale.
     Once having reached the very top, they stop
     And look, and plan the hunt in some detail.
     They all spread out across the place, and then
     To guarantee that order will prevail,
     Some take the dogs, and some the hawks in hand,
     And some stand guard, as Strozzo did command.

17. High up on both the slopes, well placed, each one
     In easy throwing range, there is a hawk.
     The third hawk goes before the kennel master

And soon it will get hurled up at a flock.
Below, there are Ulivier, Bartolo,
And more, prepared to spot a partridge cock.
Midway, in one of the more grassy places,
The trainer lets his dogs out of their traces.

18.   Just as some fiery horse will start to run,
Or fly, because the trumpet does proclaim
The starting signal of another race,
So dogs who've just been loosed will do the same.
But if their trainer doesn't draw them off,
Shaking his stick and calling some by name,
It would be hard to keep up with the pack:
Only the whip and whistle hold them back.

19.   "Hold up, good dog. Hold up and walk. Come back.
Get out of there. Come here. Hold up and walk!
Hey scalawag! Tamburo and Guerrina,
Pay heed to Staccio, see he starts to balk.
Hey lazybones, hey liar! Turn Rosina,
Good dog, watch out now for the pretty flock.
Fagiano, come, that turn was awfully weak."
In such a manner did the master speak.

20.   "Look out! ho Staccio, something whirs, it whirs:
Just what, my darling, is he trying to flush?
Though Staccio has the will and great desire,
I see he raises nothing from the brush.
Look there how Corta entertains herself.
I hear it now, the noise they'll make, the rush.
They'll leap and dance and one will scare them out,
The best dog of the pack without a doubt.

21.   "Buontempo's on its scent, he'll flush it out—
I see that he is hot upon its spoor.
Look to Buontempo, he's the one that stalks
The bird. I think I see and hear it whir.
In fact he's rather old, but never mind:
I've watched him, and I know that he can score.

My good Buontempo never errs, I've found.
Ulivier, you're on! One's on the ground!

22. "Look there! One's on the slope. I told you so,
     I heard them. Look! One's at the dried-up brook.
     Look at the vine, there's one! and one nearby,
     And two near me, and there, a thousand, look!"
     Giovan Francesco was the first to cast
     His hawk, and then with cries and shouts he shook
     The land, to make it do just what it should.
     But in his haste he failed to pull its hood.

23. "Guglielmo! There! A partridge flies toward you.
     You'll raise your hand, if you take off your hat.
     It's up to you now. Don't just stand there. Good!"
     Guglielmo casts and shouts, "Away, you rat."
     The hawk gives chase and nabs it from behind,
     And then before a soul could say "Jack Sprat"
     The hawk soars up, two hundred feet I'd say,
     Then falls to earth to pluck and tear its prey.

24. Guglielmo shouts, "Call off that dog, it wants
     To get the partridge from my hawk's sharp claws."
     He grabs a stone and throws it at Guerrina,
     And runs alone on down the slope because
     His sticks are far too short to reach the dog.
     He does not see his hawk, although he draws
     Up close, and so he stops and stands stock still
     To better hear the tinkling of its bell.

25. And standing so, he finally sees his hawk.
     "Presto," he cries, "It's done. The bird is caught."
     Elated, he walks over to the hawk
     Like one who knows this sport, who's been well taught.
     He takes it by the jess and lets it have
     The gamebird's head, which does not weigh a lot.
     Then from its claws he extricates the fowl.
     He makes it perch, and sets on it the cowl.

26.   Meanwhile Giovan Francesco has retrieved
    His hawk. He takes it to a better part
    Of that same valley. There, a bird comes straight
    At him, and when he sees the partridge start
    To come in range, he spreads his fist and casts
    The hawk, just like a master of that art.
    The hawk comes close. The partridge, old and wise,
    Escapes, and leaves the hawk without a prize.

27.   In truth this was a really worthless hawk,
    More like a kestrel, since it was so small.
    I do not think it could have caught a finch.
    In fact there was no hope for it at all
    Failing a narrow lead or early strike.
    Missing its prey, it'd soar up high to loll
    About and play. That time it lacked success
    Because it paid no heed and could care less.

28.   Foglia had meanwhile made a noble throw,
    When higher up the bank a partridge whirred
    On by. The hawk then flew across the slope
    And right in front of Foglia nabbed the bird.
    He runs on up, and since his hawk's the best,
    The taking of the bird seems quite assured.
    Onto the open ground it drags its kill,
    And there it stains with blood its claws and bill.

29.   The hawk did this because it was so young.
    Meanwhile Ulivier begins to shout:
    "Look! Call the others! Go get Capellaio!
    One of them's here," he said, "without a doubt.
    Tie up the dogs. La Rocca will suffice.
    From underneath the ground she'd draw it out.
    Guglielmo, now is not the time to fiddle.
    To Foglia! Keep la Rocca in the middle!"

30.   So this is done, and when they all are ready,
    The kennel master says, "Down Rocca, go!
    Look! Here is where it landed! Run and fetch!

Grab it! And if you do, it's yours, you know."
He asks, "Have you all really been alert?"
Just then a partridge bursts up from below.
"Foglia, to you!" He throws and makes a hoot.
Guglielmo in a hurry follows suit.

31. But Foglia's hawk gives up the chase. On fleeing
Guglielmo's hawk it now has set its will.
Guglielmo cries, "You've got it, Foglia." Though
Concealing it, he feels a certain thrill.
Then Foglia says, "Ulivier run down
Since you're so close." Guglielmo stands stone still.
But when Ulivier had run down further,
He clearly saw one hawk had caught the other.

32. Though Foglia thinks Guglielmo's hawk has his,
It's Foglia's hawk that's grabbed the other's throat.
Then Foglia says what follows to Guglielmo:
"You are indeed a rude, ill-mannered lout.
I do not think your hawk hunts partridges,
But other hawks. It's foolish to devote
One's time to hunting birds with boys like you:
Such games are most unfair, and boring too."

33. Guglielmo holds his tongue and takes great pains
To keep well hidden his elatedness:
"I did not see it, that's a certainty,"
With humble-sounding words he does confess,
And many times he makes the same reply.
But Foglia had descended with success,
And when he had approached the hawks, he found
Guglielmo's mauled, his own quite safe and sound.

34. He quickly throws the hunter's lure—the hawk
Retrieves it, no less quickly furthermore,
And Foglia pets the hawk, he pampers it
Just as one would a winner in that war.
Guglielmo meanwhile sees that he's deceived:
He sees the dying hawk is his, wherefore

He says, "It's you then, Foglia, who's the lout."
He then comes close to giving him a clout.

35. But Foglia steps aside to dodge the blow
Just as Guglielmo gestures threateningly.
The latter says, "You're crazy if you think
That I will let you out of this scot-free.
Unable to avenge this act, I think
I'd hang myself, and if I had with me
Michel or Vannuccino, you'd be led
To act quite differently, you dunderhead."

36. Foglia gets up to go—he stands there silent,
Even resigned, before this show of bile.
No different are the face and words of one
Who, counting on acquittal at a trial,
Suddenly learns that he has been condemned.
Guglielmo: "I'll be prudent for a while,
But till I breathe my last I won't forget:
We'll meet again sometime, though not just yet."

37. And now the sun draws near the midday hour:
The shadows, shortening, shrinking, aren't the same.
Their shapes appear deformed and sinister
Like the foreshortened figures painters frame.
The locust lifts the volume of its song.
The world is burning like a torch's flame.
The air is still. The leaves don't stir a jot.
It's now the season that's most fierce and hot.

38. Then spoke my Dionigi, red and sweating,
Appearing like an egg just newly laid:
"I can no longer stay. Giovan Francesco,
Come back with me. Oh, please, come to my aid!
Come all of you so we can go together.
He is a true barbarian, I'm afraid,
Who now, when all creation burns, would want
To stay here longer and pursue the hunt."

39. This said, he waits no longer for Giovan
    Francesco, but he turns his horse about,
    And since the sun is eating them alive,
    The others follow quickly in a rout.
    Next comes the kennel master and his pack
    Of panting dogs whose tongues are hanging out.
    With every step they feel the heat redouble,
    As if there's fire in every bit of stubble.

40. So both the gay and gloomy turn toward home:
    Several, with gamebags full of birds, are glad,
    While others who have none and now must find
    Some other meat are reticent and sad.
    Guglielmo, who comes last and cannot bear
    The wrong he feels, is venomous and mad.
    Giovan Francesco doesn't care a bit,
    For he still hunts just for the fun of it.

41. Once all are home the kennel master stows
    The harnesses and sets about to mind
    The dogs and put them in their stalls: the others,
    Beside the cask of cooling wine, now find
    Their floating cups, another kind of hunt
    Where no one fails or leaves his bird behind.
    The Trebbiano wine was most suspicious,
    But longing will make anything delicious.

42. Each concentrates on working his own gullet:
    The first assault takes place without a sound,
    But then they start to talk of various matters
    Once they have finished their initial round.
    Each one attempts to find some good excuse
    To tout and celebrate his hawk's renown.
    And those whose hawks had failed to do a lot
    Now vie with words and drinking from the pot.

43. Guglielmo's grudge had now begun to spoil
    Their day, so in his well-intentioned way
    Good Dionigi rises to his feet,
    And to Guglielmo he has this to say:

"Why do you want to ruin all our fun?
It's true your case seems strange, and well it may,
But do as I have done, be temperate:
I killed my hawk, and yet I do not fret."

44. Guglielmo likes the speaker, so these words,
     This gentle style, delight him a great deal.
     And since Guglielmo has a gentle heart,
     With Foglia he at last decides to heal
     The breach, whereupon he makes this humble speech:
     "I want to bear in peace the pain I feel.
     With you no longer do I want to spat."
     All go to bed, and that's the end of that.

45. And just what each will dream throughout the night,
     That would be wonderful to tell or say,
     For each, I'm sure, will make up for lost time,
     And want to sleep till nine the following day.
     But later we'll go down to yonder shore
     And make some carp forsake the waterway.
     That's how, my friend, we spent the day in pleasure,
     And sang a thousand sugared rhymes in measure.

The Partridge Hunt

Probably written in the late 1460s, "The Partridge Hunt" is one of
Lorenzo's earliest and most original poems. Hawking was Lorenzo's favor-
ite sport, and the work remains an important documentary source for our
understanding of this patrician pastime, which is portrayed in a much
more vivid and detailed way than in the treatises of the period.

The strong narrative, the humor, and the realism of the poem have been
admired by recent critics (see Sturm 36–40, Orvieto 1976, 17–21, and
Rochon 435–74). Lorenzo is unsparing in showing the pride, rivalry, an-
ger, and silliness of the falconers. He astutely shows how the hawks be-
come extensions of the will and desires of their owners, most of whom are
identifiable as historical figures and members of Lorenzo's band (*brigata*)
of friends.

There is still no general agreement on the Italian text. Generally, I have followed Bigi 1965 and Chiari. Martelli's arguments in favor of redaction B have not convinced me, but I have followed his emendation of octaves 10–12 for redaction A (he reverses the order of 11 and 12 and emends "Luigi" in 12.5 to "Lui gia"; see Martelli 1965b, 57–58).

My thanks go to John Testa, registered falconer, for help with the technical aspects of the subject. An earlier version of my translation appeared in the *Journal of the North American Falconers' Association* (1986).

1.6. *The one who loved the laurel tree of old*: that is, Apollo, the sun, who loved Daphne, later transformed into a laurel tree, a favorite image of Lorenzo's because of the association of the tree's name, *alloro*, with his own name.

2.3. *it* in the original stands for the wolf.

5.3ff. *Guglielmo*, etc.: the falconers are known from other texts as friends of Lorenzo, so, for instance, Guglielmo is Guglielmo de' Pazzi, Lorenzo's brother-in-law.

12.1. *Pulci*: The renowned poet (1432–84), author of *Morgante*, and a retainer and friend of Lorenzo. See Jordan.

31.3. *"You've got it, Foglia"*: Guglielmo pretends to think Foglia's hawk will get the partridge.

31.4. *a certain thrill*: Guglielmo secretly hopes his hawk will nab Foglia's.

35.7. *Michel or Vannuccino*: either friends or servants of Guglielmo.

41.5. *floating cups*: these are floating on top of the wine in the open vat. The hunters' haste in grabbing the cups is *another kind of hunt*.

45.7–8. *my friend*: the poem, then, is a report to one of Lorenzo's friends, who did not participate in the hunt.

Symposium (selections)

I

That time of year when all the leaves change hue
   and lay aside their green, and all the trees
   turn pale and, later, lose their foliage too;   3
then, when the peasant with his rustic ways,
   awaiting some reward for all his labors,
   looks forward to the fruit of toilsome days,   6
and reckons up his gains to get some sense
   whether the year gone by will grant him hope
   of happiness, or future indigence;   9
when one beholds in every town and street
   and every byway Bacchus, with whose spirit
   I hope this work of mine will be replete;   12
then, as so often happens, I had passed,
   outside my city, several days of leisure,
   and I was coming back to town at last.   15
To make my way less long, less roundabout
   (since I believe it's wise for one who can,
   to take the straight and shun the crooked route),   18
and see again my own beloved Fiorenza,
   I was approaching town along the road
   that leads into the portal of Faenza,   21
when I observed such throngs proceeding through
   the streets, that I won't even dare to guess
   how many men made up that retinue.   24
The names of many I could easily say:
   I knew a number of them personally,
   but did not know what sent them on their way.   27

There's one I saw among those myriads,
 with whom I'd been close friends for many years,
 as I had known him since we'd both been lads.   30
To him I turned and said, "Hey Bartolino,
 what is it drives you all abroad and at
 a pace more lively than an andantino?   33
Can I find out what longing makes you opt
 to go about? Do stay and speak to me."
 And when he heard these words of mine he stopped.   36
As when some little bird, about to glide
 into a net, takes notice of the dulcet
 tones of the other birds, then swerves aside,   39
just so with him; except he showed no taste
 for stopping, since it seemed to him hard work:
 lost ground, he knew, is not regained posthaste.   42
"For me to tell you what you want to know
 is only right, although I'm in a hurry
 as you can see, for reasons I'll now show.   45
Rifredi bridge is object of our race,
 for there Giannesse's tapped a cask of wine,
 and this is what accelerates our pace.   48
To drink with him is why we're rushing there,
 and this alone propels us through the streets
 more swiftly than a bird that cleaves the air.   51
Basa and Marco rush to satisfy
 their vulgar cravings: they are long since there,
 and you won't find them standing idly by.   54
Such insolence as theirs you've never seen
 before: they gave their word they'd take me with them,
 and that is why I'm now so full of spleen.   57
And though those two can't even tell good wine
 from bad, somehow they have the cheek to drink.
 And you can just imagine how they 'dine.'   60
So let them stay, then, on the path they chose:
 I know I'll get revenge, for one of them
 already has a leg that's varicose."   63
"Friend Bartol—who's that sitting at his leisure
 in front of Romituzzo's?" I inquired.
 And he to me, "A man who loves his pleasure.   66

And if you'd like to see how wine appalls him,
    I'll prove it to you through one thing alone:
    The Little Grape's what everybody calls him.   69
His throat, all tense and tight, the lips like chalk,
    reveal to what extent wine's laid him low,
    and also why the man can barely talk."   72
"Who's that one there with cheeks so rubicund,
    and those two with him wearing long-hemmed cloaks?"
    And he: "Each one of them's a clergyman.   75
The fat priest, from Antella, is an eater,
    and though he seems quite careless, he takes care
    to carry always with him half a liter.   78
The next one wears a smile serene and wise
    below a curious nose that's long and peaked:
    he too has made of drink his Paradise.   81
He is the Bishop of Fiesole,
    the cup he bears, the mark of his devotion,
    and with him's Ser Anton, his own curé.   84
Always, the faithful cup's in his possession,
    in every time of year, in every place,
    and even in a solemn church procession.   87
No doubt it will be always there to wait
    on him, and when he 'changes diocese,'
    the cup will rap upon the pearly gate.   90
The cup will follow him upon his bier,
    so let them put it with him in his tomb,
    that death may offer him a bit of cheer.   93
And that is what he'll ask for in his will.
    Haven't you seen him in procession give
    orders to halt, thus causing a standstill?   96
He then calls on his priests to gather round
    that they may form for him a hiding place,
    and while each canon shields him with his gown,   99
He makes his cup a cover for his face."

II

Having to laugh yet also moved by shame
   because of all the things I'd heard and seen,
   I stood there like a man who's in a dream.   3
Then someone weak from too much drinking came
   along beside me as he passed us by:
   I knew him right away, for he was lame.   6
I turned and said, "Hold up a bit, stand still!
   Hey you who scamper faster than a panther,
   stay here with me a minute if you will."   9
And that one slowed his pace, he pulled up hard,
   but like a goaded horse that's loath to stop,
   so I addressed him: "Welcome Adovard!"   12
"I am not really Adovard," said he,
   "but Thirst itself, the most distinguished thing
   that God has given to humanity,   15
the best, most precious, excellent and dear.
   Yet here a tricky question comes to light
   and doubts about my statement must appear.   18
If drinking quenches thirst, which as I say
   is good, it follows drinking must be bad;
   but we can solve the problem in this way: 21
a natural thirst like mine will not default;
   rather, the more I drink, the more my thirst
   takes fire, as if I am imbibing salt;   24
and like Antaeus, able to restore
   his strength (they say) by falling on the ground,
   my thirst, by means of drink, grows all the more; 27
and since the simple woman's water was the kind
   that kills all thirst, I choose to play it safe:
   whenever water's offered, I decline.   30
In wine is my delight, so let us go:
   it gives me joy, it gives me cheer, it is
   the single greatest good I'll ever know;   33
but when that need for which I live is dead,
   and I can feel no more the pangs of thirst,
   then take a stick and knock me on the head." 36

His words were hard to hear, his voice quite weak,
   although it used to ring out loud and clear.
     He stopped, and Bartol then began to speak: 39
"Alas, what's made that voice of yours so scrawny?"
   And he, with effort: "Most of all my former
     office, when I was dean of San Giovanni.   42
What man could keep himself from guzzling
   the consecrated wine? And though I suffer
     for all this now, I don't regret a thing: 45
I came with little voice—with less did I withdraw,
   but dying well, I won't repent a thing—
     let me repeat—I won't repent at all.   48
By dying 'on the job,' I'll rest at ease,
   for dying well does honor to one's life."
     He said no more and vanished like the breeze.   51

IV

The third one—whom you see already—studies,
   once in a while, theology: he's earned
     a doctorate—from his drinking buddies;   81
and he has comprehended that the worst
   chastisement suffered by our Lord on earth
     was when he cried out from the cross, "I thirst."   84
And if it happens, preaching, that he reads
   this text, he feels firsthand that agony,
     and then it seems his heart is torn and bleeds.   87
Yet if his learning matched his need to stuff his face,
   he wouldn't dare invoke Saint Augustine
     or Saint Jerome to buttress up his case.   90

VII

The sun had reached its midday height by now—
   which made the shadows shrink—it stood now nearly
     opposite to the Dipper and the Plow.   3

The crowd was multiplying all the same—
  no meadow grass could be as thick as was
  the swarm that had Rifredi as its aim. 6
One of that crowd was lame, his hip half-twisted,
  others had festering legs or turned-out eyelids,
  one, who had had a stroke, appeared half-witted; 9
and there were cherub cheeks the hue of roses,
  hernias that were like purses with their trusses,
  mange-eaten eyebrows, sad contorted noses. 12
I saw one group of twenty or fifteen
  together, bump and crash into each other
  like goblets floating in a wine tureen. 15
These men I knew, and they were now so near
  that they'd be grape juice, had I joined the press.
  But of the things I saw them do, now hear. 18
Sometimes two men close by would have a notion
  to talk, but all at once this couple would
  be swept apart within that surging ocean. 21
One of this crowd, on reaching us, now eyed
  my master, gave a wink and tittered. "Greetings
  to you and all your crew," my Sire replied. 24
"Much better it would be to be up there
  before the harvest starts, where you can drink
  good wine and swill it down without a care." 27
The one who'd winked said, "Sire, that's well sung."
  He chewed his words so, they weren't clear, and said
  "Enough" and could no longer move his tongue. 30
Then wanting to embrace the one who led
  my way, he turned—the swell propelled him on
  and he embraced a friend of his instead. 33
Just so a dog who struggles to traverse
  a river hopes to reach the facing shore
  but lands downstream, so strong's the current's force. 36
"Please tell me, then, these persons' names, oh Sire,
  so that I don't sound stupid when I speak,"
  I said, and he complied with my desire. 39
"The one who winked, the one you now behold—he's
  the one whose head is like a shock of fennel—
  and he's my own dear Lupicin Tedaldi. 42

Surefooted he is not, his eyes, they glisten;
   though ruddy-faced, his wings are clipped. But as
   to what these fellows did last summer, listen.   45
When with the crickets' din the world burns hotter,
   these ones, remaining seated on their stools,
   would let into their rooms three feet of water.   48
And there were many goblets, all afloat,
   unlucky though the cup that came too close:
   they'd leave it lighter than an empty boat.   51
And yet these fellows barely knew the art
   of manners, which disturbed them quite a bit
   when one of their companions loosed a fart.   54
The bubble made the water boil and fume
   and caused a squall, in consequence of which
   some goblets sank like sieves and met their doom.   57
Then Lupicino sprang up with agility
   and to his neighbor said, 'A man would rather
   stand, than sit down in your proximity.   60
If such an outrage had been perpetrated
   in our departed fathers' time, what would
   have been the fine, what would this wrong have rated?'   63
The other: 'Learn it at your own expense:
   since *you* served beans for supper, breaking wind
   became a must—so stop this insolence!   66
Let's take these cups and yield to our desire
   to drink.' But Benedetto, cup upraised,
   broke in, 'We're children, aren't we, of one sire.   69
Wine is our father, whence it will be shown
   that we should be more calm. Leonardo, you
   I'll overthrow by rational means alone.   72
If in good wine our innards are immersed,
   let's soak our outsides in the wine that spilled,
   for undiluted water kills the thirst.'   75
This speech assuaged them, settling their score.
   Their feelings soothed, my Lupicino said,
   'I love you, Benedetto, all the more.'   78
Then to Anteo, sitting at his side:
   'Let's each of us drink from the other's cup:
   a peace not pledged with wine cannot abide.'   81

And so they made their peace by drinking vino.
   If you don't know them yet, these drinkers were
   Anteo, Ercole, and Lupicino."   84
(If Benedetto's eyes look like a hawk's, sewn tight,
   it is because he's always hitting them,
   and this has nearly robbed him of his sight.)   87
Nor had they need of crabs or frog legs fried,
   or radishes or roasted beans or fennel:
   though lacking these, their thirst revivified.   90
"Let's go now, no more talking to this crew,"
   the Sire said to me. To them he said,
   "Goodbye," and they, without delay, withdrew.   93
Toward one who was an arrow's flight from us
   my gaze now turned. When he had drawn up close,
   the Sire treated him with tenderness.   96
He tried to hug this newfound bag of jelly
   without delay, but couldn't do it: neither
   of them could get beyond the other's belly.   99
Three times he tried to clasp him to his breast.
   Three times he stretched his arms in that attempt.
   Three times his hands returned to his own chest.   102
Whereupon he said, "Let's talk, if that's the way
   it has to be, as would two neighbors from
   their windows, parted by an alleyway.   105
Greetings to Stia's priest, dear friend of mine!
   Now could it be you've quitted Casentin
   to make up for a scarcity of wine?"   108
He said, "You're not all wrong in what you think.
   I'm also going to the baths so as
   to find again my long lost urge to drink.   111
Though wine enough for two I can consume,
   what's new for me is drinking twenty cups
   and feeling bloated as a big balloon.   114
A thousand nasty potions I have blended,
   so as to make me pee and rouse my thirst,
   but not a one has done the job intended.   117
And that's the reason I have taken off:
   a fever's what I seek, if only so
   the thirst might reawake my urge to quaff.   120

If this condition does not disappear,
   I'll welcome death, which couldn't be much worse."
   My Sire: "Take up the path before you here,   123
that God may give you back your missing thirst!"

VIII

As curdled milk that's carried in a cup
   by someone not so steady on his feet
   will slop around and get all shaken up,   3
just so the parson's buttocks, overwrought
   and plump, now wallow with his clumsy steps:
   sometimes he lifts his trotters, sometimes not.   6
Just as a youth, a wine glass in his grip,
   while walking, sloshes the wine, and wets the nail
   and finger hooked around the glass's lip,   9
so sloshed the parson's paunch through all its girth.
   His hose rolled round his knees, he looked for thirst,
   and pressed ahead for all that he was worth.   12
His butt looked like the backside of a deer:
   as soon as he had turned from us, we saw
   a bumper crop of lather on his rear.   15
And let me add that he was also wearing
   a sack that held a sausage, dried bone marrow,
   a wheel of salty cheese, a kippered herring,   18
and four anchovies strung up in a row—
   and all of this was stewing in his sweat:
   how to describe him better, I don't know.   21
And so the priest went on in stateliness,
   his bottom bobbed and sometimes sounded forth
   a fart, the smell of which was hard to miss.   24
A man, whose face resembled wormy tripe,
   came up. If he had sucked a straw, you'd say
   he was the spitting image of a snipe.   27
"This one's a priest whose name is Tummylove,
   and that's no accident: since he is wetter
   than a sponge, it fits him like a glove.   30

And when the Host is raised, if there's no wine
   in it, he will not kneel, for he believes
     it's been deprived of all that is divine.   33
And just as once, through God-inspired force,
   Joshua, flouting nature, stopped the sun,
     so this one and his roommate stopped the course   36
of murky Night, tenebrous and opaque.
   They mixed up darkness with the light of day.
     A miracle! Now hear of their mistake!   39
The first day, opening up a closet door,
   they thought they'd opened up a window. Seeing
     that all was dark, they went to bed once more!   42
God willed the landlord roust them out of bed
   and demonstrate to them that it was day,
     and but for this, those two might now be dead.   45
On the third day, the two were resurrected
   from the bed. Briefly up the second day,
     they slumbered nearly three days undetected."   48
And so it was the parson passed on by
   while we were carrying on this conversation.
     By then another man had caught our eye.   51
"And who is that, Ser Doughnut," I inquired,
   "that one in company with six or seven
     others who look like fellows he has hired.   54
Why is this man so ample in the rear?
   Ser Fatso, tell me why he's walking like
     a child who's crapped into his underwear.   57

. . . .

Symposium (selections)

In its earliest form, "Symposium" probably dates back to 1466–67 (Martelli 1966, 10–11), with additions and revisions in the 1470s. Like "The Partridge Hunt," the poem is humorous, contains historical personages, and is narrated by Lorenzo, or his alter ego. It is at once a satire of gluttony and excessive drinking and a parody of Dante's *Divine Comedy* and

other forms, such as the Petrarchan Triumph, which are built on an enu-
meration or list of characters. As Lorenzo strolls through Florence, his
guides or "Virgils" identify and describe the city's famous gluttons and
tipplers. The Platonic title gently twits Ficino and the Platonic Academy at
Careggi with its festive suppers. Lorenzo betrays in the poem an almost
Felliniesque fascination with grotesques and caricatures: it is the Lorenzo
who accepts his own ugly portraits and hints that Michelangelo should
chip a tooth out of his faun. But for Lorenzo the grotesqueness of the
gluttons and drunks results from their intemperance, just as beauty and
grace are, in Neoplatonism, the manifestation of a well-ordered soul. The
notorious imagery of the last capitoli is indebted to the semiscatological
punishment of the gluttons in *Inferno*: excessive eating and drinking are
discredited by dwelling on their unsavory after-products. For further com-
mentary, see my Introduction, part III, Sturm (41–48), Orvieto 1976 (21–
27), and Rochon (545–98).

I have consulted Bigi's text (1965) and Martelli's critical edition (1966)
and followed Martelli's sensible rearrangement of the last capitoli.

I.76.	*The fat priest, from Antella*: Francesco di Tommaso di Nofri.
I.82.	*The Bishop of Fiesole*: Guglielmo Becchi, a historical per- sonage like most of the other figures in the poem.
I.89.	'*changes diocese*': that is, when he dies.
II.25.	*Antaeus*: mythical giant who regained his strength when- ever he touched his mother, Earth.
II.28.	*the simple woman's water*: cf. the Gospel of John 4.6–15, where Jesus speaks to the woman at the well and com- pares his teachings to water that will prevent a person's thirst from returning.
IV.79.	*The third one*: one of the three Schiattesi brothers, also a priest.
IV.90.	*Saint Jerome*: in the Italian he is referred to simply as "he who bloodied the stone."
VII.23.	*My Master*: Lorenzo's guide, Nastagio Vespucci, father of Amerigo Vespucci. In capitolo 5, Bartolino had left Lorenzo, handing him over to this new guide, whom Lorenzo addresses as master, just as Dante the pilgrim ad- dressed Virgil in Hell.

VII.54.   *one of their companions*: Leonardo; the others are, besides
                     Lupicino, Anteo and Ercole.
VII.100–102.   *Three times*, etc.: parodies a scene in Dante's *Purgatory*
                     2.80–81. There, in vain, the pilgrim tries to embrace three
                     times a spirit.
VII.106.   *Stia's priest*: Leonardo di Ricco da Cignano.
VIII.28.   *Tummylove*: in the Italian, Arlotto or glutton. This is the
                     famous piovano (parish priest) Arlotto Mainardi (1396–
                     1484), author of the widely read *Facezie* (jokes and hu-
                     morous sayings).
VIII.57.   The poem, incomplete, breaks off here.

The Novella of Giacoppo

There has always been at Siena, as many must know, an abundance of fools and a goodly quantity of ignoramuses. I do not know whether that air naturally produces such men, or whether, since that stock had base seed to start with, it is a natural thing for it to produce fruit in keeping with its seed. And as they say that he is a good son who resembles his father, perhaps the sons, wishing not to shame their fathers, outdo themselves to behave so as not to appear bastards.

There was, therefore, not many years ago in Siena a citizen called Giacoppo Belanti, a man of about forty, quite well off, but something of a dunce. Among his other gifts of fortune, or rather of misfortune, he had a wife of great beauty, a quality which in Siena seems as natural among the women as it is for the men to have a little of the fool and braggart in them. This lady of his was about twenty-five years old, and as happens to other beautiful ladies, she was courted by a handsome young man.

The gentlewoman's name was Cassandra, and the youth, a Florentine, was called Francesco. He had been a student at Siena for a long time and in love with Cassandra during the entire period; from which state of affairs it might reasonably be supposed to follow that she was no less favorably inclined toward him than he was to her, especially when one adds that Francesco was an exceptionally handsome young man and she at present of an age to be able to tell bad from good and to know what a woman can know.

For truly that is the age at which it is good to love women; for when they are younger, most of the time they are restrained by modesty and timidity, and when they have passed this age, either they think more than is good in such situations, or because they have lost part of their natural heat, they are somewhat colder than suits the need of lovers.

Francesco had been on this lady's traces so long, without being able to lead her into the net, that he could think of nothing else day or night except how he might bring this long desire of his to a satisfying culmination. And what aroused his passion more was that he saw that only the means and the way were lacking, the parties themselves being quite favorably disposed. Although Cassandra liked him very much, her love was nevertheless held in restraint somewhat by concern for her honor, and no less by the jealousy of Giacoppo, who comported himself toward her no otherwise than most husbands who have beautiful wives are accustomed to do.

In proportion as she was beautiful, Cassandra bore these restraints less willingly, seeing herself henceforth married to an old man neither too prepossessing in appearance nor very vigorous in battle. And what gave her further reason to seek greener pastures was that she knew him to be half fool. These reasons were sufficient to kindle a fire even where there was no coal. And besides, it is a very natural thing, when one has a choice between good and bad, the sooner to choose the good; anyone who did the contrary would be adjudged insane and fit to be chained up.

And truly it seems to me that women's lot is very unfortunate, and that the men have a great advantage over them; for a man, no matter how worthless and bad he may be, can always pick a woman to his taste, or not choose her. A woman, without knowing what or how, remains at the discretion of someone else, and has to accept what she is offered in order to avoid worse; and she must congratulate herself on things which are the occasion for them of a thousand deaths a day. And therefore it is no wonder that indiscretions come to light every day which ought truly to be judged with more considerateness than they are, and we ought to be more than commonly tolerant of them, for the above reasons.

But to return to our story, Cassandra and Francesco lacked only the means to make each other happy. Their difficulty was all the more galling to them in that they felt they were losing the match to a fool, who was the only one standing in their way, although Giacoppo deprived them of the possibility of contenting themselves more by his anxiety than by abundance of intellect. Francesco had gone over the matter in his mind again and again, and finally, deciding to rely upon Giacoppo's simplicity, he worked out the following scheme.

In the first place, he made a show of completely abandoning his love for Cassandra. When this act had gone on for some time, so that Giacoppo already felt almost secure about him, he one day feigned that he had received a letter from certain relatives of his in Florence, who informed him that they had picked a wife for him. This rumor spread first among his friends and companions and soon was known through most of Siena, where he was well known and liked. And among others, it came back to the ear of Giacoppo, who was as happy as could be at the news, assuming that he might feel completely secure about his wife, since he believed that Francesco would either have to leave Siena or at least take his mind off those things which had formerly preoccupied it, as taking a wife customarily leads some men to do.

When Giacoppo was free of all suspicion, Francesco began to say that under no circumstances did he wish to leave Siena, for he had already put in so much study and effort up to that time, that he did not wish to abandon his work just as he was about to obtain his doctorate. He had therefore decided to bring his wife to Siena and maintain her there until he had accomplished, in his own good time, what he had come for. Upon this he rented a house, not very near Giacoppo's, but in a place where Giacoppo very often passed by. Here he planned to come to live with his wife, as his previous quarters were insufficient for him and the lady. Not long after, he announced that he was going to Florence to get married and to bring his wife to Siena. And thus he did.

When he got to Florence, he sought out a prostitute, one of those who carry on the art more discreetly, but not less, than the public ones. She called herself Meina, a pet name for Bartolomea; she was quite pretty in face and in general appearance and lived in the quarter called Borgo Stello. He came to an agreement with her by which, in return for a certain sum, she was to accompany him for some time. She was completely agreeable to this, and Francesco, accompanied by a respectable entourage, brought her to Siena, telling everyone that she was his wife. All accepted this as true, so that she was very honorably taken up by the gentlewomen of Sienese society and received many invitations. As one versed in cunning and evil, she knew very well how to cover up her innumerable stains under a fine and ladylike exterior, and to appear very moral and most averse to any form of vice.

She had been tutored by Francesco in what she had to do, and so began to stand occasionally at the window, which, as we have said, opened over a street through which our Giacoppo had to pass very often on his business errands. Noticing her often at the balcony, he one day, to his misfortune, threw her a glance; she in turn gave him a favorable look, and smiled at him, causing to arise in him, although it was well beyond the season, a desire for May figs; and he began to say to himself: "Francesco courted my wife for so long and never succeeded in obtaining even a warm look from her, as young and handsome as he is; this lady is so pretty, and I, old as I am, within so short a time am already making headway with her. It looks as though it may happen with Francesco as with Mainardo's dog, who leaped to bite and was himself bitten first."

And spurred as much by vanity as by desire, he began to pass by more and more often; and finding the terrain better disposed every day he often boasted in a circle of young men, saying: "The fact of the matter is that old men really know the art. You spend all the time of your lives standing around wishing, and never get anywhere; whereas I, as old as you see me, a little while ago ran into a certain stroke of luck which any of you would pay his eyes for. I think I have said enough."

But for all these words, he still could not find a means or way of arriving at confession with her. Finally, since the initiative did not appear from him, Bartolomea, as the lady now called herself for greater decorum and to remain unknown, had to send a letter to him through one of her maids. In it she said that she was dying for him, and that, so God help her, she feared he had cast a spell over her. Giacoppo could not contain himself for joy at this event, and he sent her a reply as ridiculous as might be expected from him.

Not much time intervened before she, having first made a show of the utmost diffidence in carrying out the intrigue, gave him a rendezvous for a certain night, saying that Francesco had gone to stay at an estate of his with a companion from Siena. When the evening, which seemed to him to tarry a thousand years, finally came, Giacoppo gave the prearranged signal and found himself in the house. Bartolomea, omitting none of the little mannerisms characteristic of one aflame with great love, led him into a bedroom and put him under the bed, telling him that he would have to stay there until a certain maid had gone off to sleep, because she wanted things kept secret. This he did, and he stayed there about two and a half hours.

When Bartolomea came back she expressed regret at his discomfort and bade him be patient with her. When they were together, Bartolomea began to roll her eyes wildly, and saying that she was driven by her affection, at one moment she would scratch his face and at another bite him so hard that she left marks. He believed that this was the way of lovers, and not only bore all quietly and patiently, but it seemed to him he was touching heaven with his finger.

Coming then to the end which is so desired and for which lovers endure so much, he, despite his age, put forth a great effort, and with much strain and toil arrived where he wished to go, etc. She feigned amazement that at his age he should give so good an account of himself, and led the poor man on to struggle to the death to accomplish what in no way appeared possible for him. And in conclusion, returning home more dead than alive, all battered and worn out, but convinced he was returning from paradise, he had to go through another battle with his wife; and in order to justify himself he had to accomplish in one night what at another time was not only difficult, but impossible for him in a year.

Bartolomea, instructed by Francesco, who did not wish the game to be lost when it was in his hands, continued to entice him. And although he went there often, he accomplished nothing much more than to return home well scratched and bitten. And thus he did many times, and the affair lasted many months, no less fine in words than in deeds, for, motivated by self-conceit, he did nothing but boast of this happiness of his among young men and old, not realizing that he was weaving the net in which he himself was to be taken.

Things had gone along in this way for some time, when Lent arrived, and Bartolomea begged Giacoppo to grant her a holiday, at least during these holy days, saying that it was time to concern themselves for their souls, even though it was difficult for her to have to remain without him for a time. These words moved Giacoppo to go to confession and avow his sins. His long-time confessor was a Franciscan friar named Fra Antonio della Marca, with whom Francesco had arranged in advance what he was to do, knowing that he was Giacoppo's confessor. Fra Antonio consented without much difficulty to Francesco's requests, even though he was a friar, feeling it was his duty to succor the afflicted by the seven works of mercy and wishing to prove that proverb true which says that there is no trap or treachery without one of that order involved in it.

When Giacoppo therefore appeared at his feet to confess himself, he began the customary questioning. When they came to the sin of lechery, Giacoppo began to relate to him his affair with Francesco's wife, as he conceived it. At this the friar grew stern and said: "Alas, Giacoppo, how could the diabolical powers have worked so strongly on you to lead you into this irremissible sin? A sin which under no circumstances is within my authority or the Pope's or even Saint Peter's, if he came alive, to absolve." Said Giacoppo: "O, I have heard it said that there is no sin so great that it can not be absolved." To this Fra Antonio replied: "That is true; but for that it is necessary to do something that I know you will never do." "To save my soul," said Giacoppo, "there is nothing I would not do, even to selling myself and my wife." Fra Antonio then said: "If that is your mind, I will tell it to you; but to me it seems certain that you will promise it and not keep your promise." Giacoppo said: "Really, you make me marvel at you; I love my soul more than anything in this world."

"Very well," said Friar Antonio, "I will tell it to you. Have you not heard it said that the sin of slander, and of things which a man retains unjustly, cannot be pardoned without restitution? That is the case here; for having taken away the honor of that young woman and her husband, your sin is unpardonable unless you make her husband, or if she does not have a husband her nearest relative stay with your wife, if you have one, and if you have no wife, with your nearest relative, as many times as you have gone to stay with his. As we read, when David committed the sin of adultery, he gave his wife to the one with whose wife he had committed it, and in this way it was pardoned him; so that you see what you have to do."

When Giacoppo heard the words of the priest, he did not feel too well, and he said to himself: "Now I see that it is I who am turning out to be Mainardo's dog." Turning to the friar, he said: "My spiritual father, even though it seems very difficult to me, I know I ought to love my soul more than anything else in this world; and I ought not to feel any shame about it at all, since David, who was a king, did it, and I am but a citizen of Siena. So that by all means, before anything else, I wish to save my soul."

The friar, hearing the devout words of Giacoppo, without a word, embraced him and kissed him on the forehead; and holding him for a while, he said: "My spiritual son, I see that the grace of God has illumined you; and I see you proceeding by a path which will lead to a successful issue. May you be blessed a thousand times. I see now that the matter will go well, thanked be the Savior. I point out to you, however, that this sin is so great, that in spite of all this, it cannot be absolved without special penance; I have therefore decided that you shall make your way unto Rome itself, for the atonement of this and your other sins. And by this way does one enter into the glory of life eternal and our life here become a joyful passage. Go then, blessed son, and carry out what you have promised me." And he gave him his benediction.

Giacoppo rose from the priest's feet and returned home full of heavy thoughts. After a great inner debate, his conscience finally won out, and he decided to go find Francesco, to restore his honor to him. Thereupon there sprang up before him another difficulty, namely, that he did not know in what manner to broach this to Francesco without great danger to himself. However, having found the means to salvation, and being under the sway of his conscience, and since it seemed to him he could do it more safely during these holy days than at another time, he one day sought out Francesco with these words: "Francesco, I have always loved you as a son, which by your age you might well be. Now then, sinfulness has led me to do a thing of which I repent me very much; and I beg you, that as God may pardon me it, you too may be willing to pardon me; and before I proceed further, promise me and swear not to hurt me, but by the passion of Our Lord, to let pass an injury which I have done you." Said Francesco: "I have always revered you as a father, I promise you on my faith, first of all for love of God, considering the season in which we are, and then for love of you, to pardon you any offense you may have committed against me." Giacoppo threw himself at his feet and said: "I will not tell it to you except on my knees."

With great difficulty Francesco succeeded in making him get up, and prepared to hear what he, much better than the speaker, knew already. And when Giacoppo had told his tale with many tears, Francesco, appearing greatly disturbed, said: "You had good foresight to make me pledge my word; if not for that, before you had left me, I would have done something which, when it was done, would not have been very pleasant for you, nor for that strumpet of a wife of mine, nor to me myself. But I care more for my soul than you did for me; and now, in few words, I pardon you everything. But now remove yourself from before me."

Giacoppo, who felt he had accomplished not a little, said: "You must stay to hear four more words and to help me obtain pardon for this sin from God." And he added that Francesco had to go and consort with his wife. To which Francesco replied: "This I did not promise you; I do not wish to be, like you, a villain and a traitor. It is enough if I have pardoned you so great an injury. And do not speak to me about it, as I wish to hear none of it; and again I tell you to remove yourself from in front of me, for you obstruct my path."

Giacoppo, fearing to make things worse, took himself off and returned to the friar. When he told the latter how the matter had gone, and when he came to the part where Francesco under no circumstances would listen to reason and allow himself to be persuaded to go and consort with his wife, the friar said: "O, this is nothing; you must make restitution of his honor to him in this way; otherwise it is as though you had done nothing." Giacoppo, not knowing how to approach Francesco again, said to the friar: "Perhaps it would be better if you sent for him a little. I will stand by and you can give him to understand how it is not a sin; and perhaps to you he will grant what he has been unwilling to grant to me."

To this the friar replied: "That is a good idea; however, I am not acquainted with him. I will give you one of my younger brethren; you can point him out from a distance, and thus it will not appear that I am sending for him especially for this." Agreeing on this procedure, Giacoppo departed with the young friar, to whom he pointed Francesco out, and the boy delivered his message. Francesco giving no outward sign, came to the church and found the friar in a small anteroom before his cell. There they made a show of carrying on a great noisy argument, laughing a good while together over the joke. Then, calling Giacoppo over to them, the friar said to Francesco: "You must by all means console this poor unfortunate Giacoppo; not for love of him, for he does not merit it, but for love of Messer Jesus, who will in turn bestow his grace on you and not impute as a sin what you do for love of His name. And I, as well as Giacoppo, will be obliged to you."

At these words Giacoppo threw himself at his feet and began to plead with Francesco to go and sleep with his wife. Francesco, pretending to weep from compassion, said: "All right, then! I agree; I wish to make of this injury and of this grace, which I am conceding to you, a gift to God, and to do for love of Him what you ask of me, even though it is most difficult for my conscience."

Giacoppo, completely happy with this answer, now began to struggle with another quandary; this was, how was his wife to be made to agree? Nevertheless, feeling confident that he could persuade her to do whatever he wished, he went home; and on the way he thought he had worked out a fine cunning scheme for becoming a cuckold. It was as follows: as soon as he entered the house, he would begin to lament bitterly, so that his wife would have reason to ask him why he was weeping. And this scheme, as he had planned it, worked out precisely, for she began to ask him, with great insistence, the reason for so many tears. To this Giacoppo replied: "I weep for I have good reason to, namely, that I am damned and cannot save my soul."

The lady, who was in on the trick, began to lament louder than he, and said: "Alas! How did this happen? What have you done? O, is there no remedy at all?" "Yes," said her husband, "but it is difficult." To which Cassandra answered: "Why do you not say what it is? If there is anything that can be done, let us do it." "I will tell you what it is," said Giacoppo. "On what you do depends whether I am saved or damned," and he began to explain the situation to her. When he came to the part about what it was necessary for her to do, she became very indignant; and, to be brief, he had to implore this grace of her on bended knee.

After he had gotten her to agree, he went at once, in order to be shriven sooner, to Francesco, and said to him: "This evening will be a good time; come to dine with me, and then, in the name of God, you can begin to help me atone for this great sin of mine." Francesco, happier than ever, put on a look as though receiving most distasteful news, and gave him clearly to understand what a singular favor he was bestowing upon him. Nor for all this did the night seem to him less than a thousand years in coming; and when it finally did arrive, he went to Giacoppo's house, where he dined abundantly, and then, leaving Giacoppo in the room, he went with his long-desired Cassandra into the bedroom and then to bed. And it should be evident to everyone that things went differently than they had gone between Giacoppo and Bartolomea.

Afterwards it was necessary, in order to atone for the remainder of the sin, for Francesco to return again and again. And later, when Giacoppo went in penitence to Rome, as he had been ordered to do by the friar, it was a rare night that Francesco did not spend with Cassandra. And thus their long love reached its culmination, and may it please God to grant to ours the same conclusion.

And so the jealous Giacoppo had to beg on naked knees, as a boon, what Francesco wanted more than anything in the world, in order to be absolved of a trespass for which he underwent the penitence before the sin. All this thanks to Friar Antonio, who behaved as some religious are wont to do; for as they are many times the source of infinite good, so at times are they as well the authors of many great evils, because of the excessive faith men unjustifiably place in them.

Translator unknown

The Novella of Giacoppo

This witty tale in the manner of Boccaccio was probably written in 1469 or 1470. Giacoppo may well be based on a real person, Giacoppo Bellanti of Siena, whom Lorenzo knew (Bigi 1965). For the influence of this novella on Machiavelli's play *La Mandragola*, see Orvieto 1976, 62–63.

This fine translation appeared anonymously in the collection edited by Valency and Levtow. I am grateful to them and to the Putnam Publishing Group for permission to reprint this translation (which conforms to the text in Bigi, 1965).

The Supreme Good

I

Lured on, escorted by the sweetest thoughts
  I fled the bitter storms of civic life
    to lead my soul back to a calmer port;   3
and so my heart was carried from that life
  to this one—free, serene, untroubled—which
    retains the little good the world still knows.   6
To free my feeble nature from the load
  that wearies it and stops it flight, I left
    the pretty circle of my native walls.   9
And having reached a pleasant shady glen
  within the shadow of that mountain which
    in its old age preserves its ancient name,   12
there, where a verdant laurel cast some shade
  below that lovely peak, I found a seat,
    my heart untrammeled by a single care.   15
And over to my left, a limpid spring
  poured forth its sweet refreshing stream,
    watering the mead that lay in front of me.   18
Shot through the fresh green grass were brilliant reds
  and whites from every kind of bloom, and in
    that loveliness I lay my weary body;   21
as many sweetly smelling fragrances
  were there as those the Phoenix gathers up
    when she begins to feel the throes of death. 24
In such a charming place I can't believe
  the air is ever turbulent, or that
    foul weather or bad luck could cause you harm. 27

So all alone in that delightful haunt,
   content to be in my own company,
   surrounded only by my own sweet thoughts,   30
I gazed out on the land—and then I heard
   a bagpipe sounding with such loveliness
   the piper's flock of sheep joined in the dance.   33
He'd come to take his nap in the cool shade
   close by that purling brook, but seeing me
   the man was filled with wonder and dismay.   36
He stopped a moment, then recovering
   his courage, with a rustic salutation
   he greeted me and so began to speak: 39
"Tell me, what purpose brings you here? Why have
   you left your theaters, your spacious halls
   and temples? Why do goat paths please you more?   42
Pray tell, what do you ponder in these groves?
   Diversions, riches, pomps? Perhaps you want
   to prize these more by studying our plight?"   45
And I to him: "I do not know of riches
   or honors sweeter than this life of yours—
   one free of all political intrigue.   48
Among you happy shepherds and you cowherds
   no hatred reigns or wicked treachery,
   and in these pastures no ambition grows.   51
Here one can gain the good and not rouse envy:
   your greed has shallow roots and you're content
   delighting in the pleasures of repose.   54
And here one says just what he means, the tongue
   does not oppose the heart—not so with us
   where he who lies the best is happiest.   57
In lucid air like this, no mouth that smiles
   conceals a heart that sighs—not so with us
   where he is deemed more wise who has more wiles.   60
With us, who trusts in simple honesty
   gets called a fool, while those who nest inside
   those walls regard the swindler as a sage,   63
and friendship's measured by expediency.
   Imagine then how sweet that love must be
   which chance alone can sap and vitiate.   66

How ever can a heart that avarice
  afflicts and fills with such outrageous hopes,
    or such excessive fears, discover peace?   69
But dwelling in these mountains, you are not
  subjected to confusing, vicious thoughts—
    your minds are not obsessed by what's in vogue.   72
Sweet fruits appease your hunger, cooling streams
  allay your thirst, and all your longings are
    fulfilled in harmony with nature's needs.   75
In summertime your bed's a pile of leaves—
  in winter there's dry hay inside a hut
    that gives you shelter from the frost and rain.   78
And though your clothes are not like those sought out
  in foreign lands beyond the salty waves,
    you're just as happy wearing shaggy hides.   81
How sweet your sleep, devoid of any cares,
  among these branches where the murmurings
    of mountain streams sigh answers to your snores. 84
The sylvan nymphs must often gather round
  this charming spring to sing in harmonies
    far lovelier than any earthly sound.   87
To this sweet stream of song, so delicate
  and bright, to bagpipe tunes and your own lays,
    the nightingale and other birds reply.   90
And when it happens that two bullocks fight,
  you're no less pleased, I think, than those who watch
    the savage sports inside our stadiums.   93
Then you, as judge, confer the leafy crown
  upon the winner, while the loser stands
    there, sad, despised, and overcome by shame.   96
Happy is he whose wants reflect his needs,
  but woe to him whose ever-hungry mind
    cannot possess the thing it covets most;   99
our boundless longing never dies but grows,
  and growing racks us all the more: who yearns
    the most must always settle for much less.   102
That man who's pleased with what he has seems much
  more rich to me than he who values what
    he doesn't have above the things he owns.   105

True wealth is tranquil poverty, so long
   as it supplies life's needs. If you feel rich
   or poor, it's what you're used to, nothing more.   108
I'll never fathom those who praise a man
   whose thought reflects what others think, but damn
   a mind content in its autonomy.   111
Your life, oh shepherd, seems to me the one
   that most approaches human peace, if that
   can still be found in this, our fallen world."   114
The shepherd did not listen any more
   but sometimes looked around distractedly
   as if to say he longed again to speak.   117
Heaving a heartfelt sigh, he then began:
   "What error makes you think it happy, such
   a life, or rather, such a martyrdom?   120
How can it please you, what you praise? And why,
   once having praised it, must you give it up?
   Why not secure this peace, then, for yourself?   123
Why do you veil the truth in such illusions?
   If truth you know, take up this truth that so
   consumes you, live the life you say you crave.   126
There's quite a difference, though, between the thought
   and deed: the path that looks so fair at first
   may turn out thorny when you take it up.   129
Is there one thing this life does not make sad?
   Like beasts we are exposed to sweltering heat
   and cold. And that's the sweetness we enjoy.   132
In snowy winter weather, cold and raw,
   you'll sometimes notice on our mantles icy
   crystals encasing every tuft of fur.   135
At times a ruthless wind molests you so
   that when you try to hide from it behind
   a rock, the savage gale still seeks you out.   138
Our feather beds are hard-packed earth or stone.
   To help restore our strength when we are weak
   we eat the food that forest creatures eat.   141
And when a wolf deprives me of a lamb,
   you will not see me suffer less than you
   when you have lost some splendid, rich estate.   144

Nor would you suffer more than I although
  your loss might seem much greater: small things count
  the same for me as great ones do for you.   147
It's in these little things that Fortune flaunts
  her power over me: withholding them
  she brings me misery beyond compare.   150
So if I lose a wood or earthen pot,
  I mourn no less than you would mourn if you
  had lost a golden bowl whose worth seems more.   153
The different values placed on wood and gold
  come not from nature but from us who judge
  that one's of precious worth, the other poor.   156
I love my crock as much as you your bowl,
  so Fortune hurts us equally: each pines
  for his own pot with like intensity.   159
The world, I think, agrees that Fortune is
  relentless, full of hate: she crucifies
  each one of us upon the cross we make.   162
I'm just a shepherd, but I know this ancient
  maxim: with his own life no man's content—
  each thinks the other's life more fortunate.   165
I'll stay where I am destined to remain,
  and you, where your own star may summon you.
  And we are not alone—all men condemn   168
their fate, no matter *where* it stations them."

II

My ears, all heedful of his words, were then
  attracted to another voice which seized
  and bound them with its sweeter harmonies.   3
I thought that Orpheus was back on earth,
  or he whose noble tones had walled up Thebes,
  so sweetly did his lyre sound to me.   6
"Perhaps that Lyre set within the sphere
  of the fixed stars fell down from heaven's realm," I said.
  "The starry sky must miss its constellation;   9

or maybe, as that ancient sage once taught,
   the transposed soul of one of these was put—
   such was his destiny—inside this player."   12
And while my eye, led on by what my ear
   could hear, looked through the boughs and leafy fronds
   to find out where such sweetness had its source,   15
behold! the eye, the noble mind, the ear,
   all in an instant heard and grasped and saw
   the one who played, his teaching, and his lyre: 18
Marsilio of Montevecchio,
   he in whom heaven poured its every grace
   that he might be a mirror to all men;   21
ever the lover of the sacred muses,
   no less is he the lover of true wisdom,
   so that the two may never be disjoined.   24
This man was like a father to us both—
   deserving as he was of every homage,
   we both stood up, delighted he was there.   27
And he, no less delighted, halted by
   that lovely fountain; settling on a rock,
   he left off playing and began to speak: 30
"I was already tired from my walk:
   some gracious god then steered my steps to reach
   this place where now I rest and am refreshed.   33
But first things first: Hail Lauro! Hail Alfeo,
   among wise shepherds surely the most wise,
   and owing to your age, my worthy father.   36
Shepherd, I'm not surprised that you are here:
   we've often met each other at this spring,
   and now and then beneath some shady beech.   39
It does amaze me greatly, though, to find
   you, Lauro, on this wooded mountain slope,
   not that your presence doesn't bring me joy.   42
Who counseled you to leave your native city?
   You know the burdens your familial
   and civic duties put upon your shoulders."   45
And I to him: "The things of which you speak
   bring on such agony that the mere thought
   of them enfeebles me and makes me grieve.   48

I've fled, a while, those vexing public cares
  in order to refresh my soul by pondering
  the pastoral way of life, a life I envy.   51
The burden of our life's unbearable:
  though *he* will disagree, I'd give the palm,
  comparing both, to this the pastoral life.   54
Such was the subject of our argument
  until we heard your lyre's dulcet tones
  which put a sudden stop to our dispute.   57
Now then, since God has granted us your presence,
  tell us, which one has strayed from the true path
  and if our lives possess authentic good.   60
But if our lot prevents our knowing good,
  then say what sort of life it would adorn,
  and if it's of this world, or is divine.   63
Each art, each science, every daily act
  and choice goes back, it seems, to this same good,
  as every stream flows back into the sea.   66
But you should tell us what this good might be:
  since you know what it is, untie this knot
  that keeps the heart bound up in such distress."   69
Marsilio to us: "I must then turn my heart
  to where your hearts have turned and are engrossed,
  however difficult this task may prove: 70
the one who grasps the truth can better know
  where truth is not than understand what it
  might be, wrapped up in such obscurity.   75
But love will greatly lighten such a load:
  to true love you must not refuse a thing,
  for they who truly love become as one.   78
Before all else I'll say, let none whose soul
  is bound and fettered by the senses think
  that he will find the true and perfect good.   81
This law was made by Him who rules supreme,
  that mortals, blind and erring, might not fix
  their thoughts exclusively upon this world.   84
Mistaking the true way, their vision of
  the good askew, what would these mortals do
  were they to think this life might yield the good?   87

Authentic good is one, no more, no less,
   and it is kept, it seems, by God, who holds
   it as a prize for those who've led good lives.   90
Thus overweening men who want to find
   the good before it's time, endure the fate
   of those who gather fruit that's still unripe.   93
If they then eat the unripe fruit, it tastes
   so sour, their teeth are set on edge, whereupon
   they usually abandon the attempt.   96
Nor do they learn how sweet the fruit becomes:
   discouraged in their first attempt, they fall
   more deeply into error day by day.   99
But drawing out this point will bore us all:
   nor do I wish to share the fate of those
   who hold that heaven's like a stretched-out pelt.   102
And so I say this good, this precious thing,
   sought and described by now in many tongues,
   is treasured up by God in his celestial choir   105
where each and every passion is annulled;
   yet since so many "goods" are counterfeit,
   we'll first divide them in the following way: 108
For those who think, there come to mind three kinds
   of good available to man." And so
   began the one who could untie this knot.   111
"The first sort Fortune gives and takes away;
   second are goods that nature gives the body;
   and third are those encompassed by our soul.   114
The goods that Fortune brings are four in all:
   dominion, riches, honor, and goodwill
   (and these last two arouse the same concern).   117
The more dominion spreads, the greater is
   the fear it breeds, and as it rules more men,
   so must hostility to it increase.   120
Caesar, it seems, named this the sovereign good,
   but then he finally saw that greater sway
   will only make you subject to more men.   123
Next is possession of great wealth, but since
   this craving's never satisfied, it keeps
   a man from ever finding any peace.   126

Worse still, men praise this evil as a good,
   and some quite foolishly put trust in that
   which often brings more harm than benefit.   129
No man desires gold for its own sake
   but for some other end, and so it's not
   the perfect good that Midas thought it was.   132
Honor, which seems so glorious and fair
   that many fools assign the good to it,
   is not the sovereign good of which I speak.   135
That is no good, what others can control,
   for all depends on him who honors you
   and praises much, not knowing whom or why. 138
Indeed, the more the ignorant mob outnumbers
   those who are wise, then so much less will he
   be known, who merits greater fame and praise. 141
Often a man is wrongly praised or blamed;
   or praised without his knowing it: for him
   it is as if there'd been no praise at all.   144
This, then, is not that true and perfect joy
   which long ago some blind men coveted,
   their minds enveloped in this false ideal.   147
And he who took goodwill to be the finest
   flower was wrong; so he was wont to think
   who in his reign endowed the world with peace. 150
Goodwill, however, is no less at risk
   than honor: someone must confer goodwill—
   that someone still can take goodwill away.   153
From this we see how vain it is to set
   one's heart on goods unreasoning Fortune rules:
   each one of them will fail and disappear.   156
From morn till night, blind, unrelenting Fortune
   brings us these specious goods and carries them
   away. No wise man ever sets his thoughts   159
or hopes where cruel Fortune has her sway.

III

"Whatever Fortune holds within her sway,"
   the newborn Plato said, addressing us,
      "cannot, therefore, be called the perfect good.   3
That good belonging to the well-formed body
   is parceled out in three essential traits:
      robustness, glowing health, and comeliness.   6
The first two, ravaged by some small complaint,
   give up those benefits in which the robust Milo
      was once so pleased to see the sovereign good.   9
But happiness was never found in these.
  . Nor will there ever be a peaceful port
      for mortals born to loveliness and grace.   12
Herillus placed in these the highest good:
   though he embodied every charm, you can't,
      for all of that, conclude he was content.   15
If you are destined to be beautiful,
   your beauty will without a doubt prove much
      more valuable to others than to you.   18
Nature confers, and can withdraw, this good,
   nor can you place your hopes in it, for it
      is like the flower thieving time devours."   21
Then leaving this idea, he went on,
   "Perhaps the good's within our mind, which can't
      be reached by others, only by ourselves.   24
The goods our souls possess when we're alive
   have been apportioned by the sages in
      two parts, the rational and sensible.   27
Our reason holds the part that is divine,
   the part we share with creatures is the senses,
      which we engage in two distinctive ways.   30
Your senses, first of all, are ordered so
   that they perform their duties perfectly,
      and, second, they procure for you delights.   33
In this was Aristippus led astray
   by specious reasoning: he aimed too low,
      embracing what was bad in both domains.   36

Some other species are our betters here,
    for certain of their senses are more keen
    than those of our harassed and tired soul.   39
The beasts, it seems, should then be happier,
    but one must add that keenness of the senses
    provokes distaste more often than delight.   42
More bad exists than good, so most of what
    we smell, discern, and taste will rouse disgust.
    No good I know can counteract this woe.   45
Sensual delights create eternal war:
    preceded by a lust that wastes the heart,
    they're governed and accompanied by doubt,   48
and followed by regrets when pleasure's fled.
    And while these carnal cravings last, the heart,
    for ardor's sake, will yearn and rage.   51
For what we drink is only sweet to us
    so long as thirst allures and snares the taste.
    If it gives out, our pleasure follows suit.   54
No thing will dare embrace its opposite:
    a state where pleasure is suffused with pain
    is thus an evil rather than a good.   57
With that, we will dismiss the sensual
    and treat what those with good recall will know
    is lovelier, the part that's rational.   60
Beneath this heading are two different limbs,
    the natural and acquired faculties,
    and that's how reason is divided up.   63
The first emerge with life itself—from them
    each mortal gets a light and certain seeds
    the instant that his soul receives its body.   66
Memory, boldness, and sagacity
    are good or evil instruments depending
    on how they're used, with evil ways or good. 69
Indeed, the more mature they are, the more
    they weigh upon the soul if badly used,
    which usually is the case in our blind world. 72
The goods that we acquire in our lives
    fall likewise into two specific kinds,"
    and so we climbed from one grade to the next, 75

"the active virtues and the meditative,
   the second being much more eminent.
   With those that are more lowly we'll begin.   78
Only the active, moral virtues teach
   the art of living in the world—they also
   serve to prepare us for the other kind.   81
This was the path of Zeno and his sect,
   and that of all the Cynic rabble too,
   who claimed that our true end was active good.   84
Nature did not extend to them more light
   than this, and what they said was easier
   to say, perhaps, than put into effect.   87
These active goods can only be attained,
   it seems, through sweat, fatigue, and hard travail:
   thus reason holds that they are incomplete.   90
In practice, temperance and fortitude
   are heavy loads to bear: the more these goods
   engender pain, the greater they're esteemed.   93
The aim of every human task, it seems,
   is toil—not for toil's sake, but for
   the peace that toil finally brings the soul.   96
It seems, therefore, quite wrong to say that our
   true end lies in these goods, which must appeal
   to their own pain for benefits they seek.   99
But why must we continue in this vein?
   That One who leads the way to our true end
   has given us His word—so follow it.   102
The Magdalen took up the better part,
   for each must choose one of two different ways.
   The way that Martha chose is fraught with cares.   105
This is the truth that never suffers change:
   no mortal can escape its just decree,
   and everything opposing it is false.   108
This Martha, as you see, is not the one
   to slake our thirst, so long enduring. Only
   the water asked for by the woman of   111
Samaria will do—so drink of that.
   Let's follow Mary, she who sat in peace,
   without a care, beside those blessed feet.   114

Like her, the mind in contemplation rests:
   when good approaches one who's in this state,
   his only longing is to contemplate.   117
It's then that one is granted health. But since
   some mortals pay this matter scant regard,
   it too will be apportioned in three parts.   120
First, we can contemplate all earthly things
   and nature; second, all that's in the sky;
   and third, the realm that lies beyond the stars.   123
Democritus did not transcend the first:
   nature, he held, creates by chance all things,
   and those to come, and ever keeps this guise.   126
He claimed that every single thing the world
   contains, without exception, was in fact
   created from the multitude of atoms.   129
But since true good is not below the moon,
   it can't reside in contemplating things
   that, one by one, decay or come undone.   132
The study of the fair celestial realm
   is not, as Anaxagoras the great
   had wished it, gladly gazing at the sky   135
and stars, the sovereign good. A higher good
   deprived it of this palm and gathered to
   itself the glory of these lesser realms.   138
And as the sun appears to cloak the stars,
   just so this shining radiance, a work
   more worthy, puts the lesser in the shade.   141
The contemplation of what dwells beyond
   the stars is worthier, the rarer that
   it is—so held exalted Aristotle,   144
philosopher whom all the world reveres.
   Such contemplation, though, is of two kinds:
   one that our souls still practice in the flesh,   147
and one this life of ours can't give. It seems
   that Aristotle placed the highest good
   in the first kind, and made no more distinctions.   150
He said, to those who grasp his writing well,
   that happiness must be the exercise
   of perfect virtue in a perfect life.   153

But if true good has two essential parts,
   the one, our will, the other intellect,
      these two together cannot be fulfilled   156
because the mind, bound up inside the flesh,
   can never comprehend the good—confined,
      it always yearns to soar to greater heights.   159
It's always anxious, filled with ever more
   impassioned longing for the good it lacks:
      through intellect, the mind's confusion grows.   162
Accordingly, our intellect and will
   become worn out: thus truth, unblemished, white
      and fair, will never by the soul be found   165
while this, our living carcass, weighs it down."

IV

With dulcet pipe I've set my verse to music,
   without the help of any other god
      than Pan, whose favor has sustained this song—   3
that Pan whom every shepherd venerates,
   whose name is feted through Arcadia,
      whose rule is over all that's born and dies.   6
But when a light's most bright to mortal eyes
   and at its most intense, it will appear
      to be less visible and more obscure.   9
This happens to the soul—like certain beasts
   the soul sees poorly all that is most bright—
      and to our eyes when they observe the sun.   12
Just so, that eye inside our mind, because
   it is imperfect, can't distinguish well
      whatever is most plain and manifest.   15
No higher can our mortal feet aspire:
   another's needed to discern the way,
      to raise our earthbound spirit to the sky.   18
Let her come forth, the mighty Thunderer's daughter,
   who issued from his head without a mother;
      let her extend her hand to my base mind.   21

May she inflame my will with holy love,
   illuminate my mind with such a light
   as he would need who longs to speak of God.   24
And since this sacred goddess has no mother,
   let our intelligence be purged of matter,
   and separate itself from all that's flesh.   27
Let her reveal the true and certain path,
   let her be to my intellect a sun,
   dispelling darkness and perplexity.   30
But now, my Muse, invoked by me so often
   but feeling she's been cast aside, laments,
   and wants to charge me with ingratitude.   33
Oh Muse, dictate to me the words and verses
   so that the light provided by Minerva
   will thus be written down as it's revealed.   36
If you, Apollo, still do love the chaste
   locks of your much-desired Daphne, help
   then him in whom her lovely name endures,   39
and grant to me from your own sacred furor
   not the amount that I myself may need
   but what the subject of my song demands.   42
Now let your favor wax, the more my wit
   falls short, that I may show Marsilio's thoughts
   in verse as I perceive them in my mind.   45
Marsilio, who looked on us with joy,
   then spoke: "We see, Alfeo father, Lauro,
   my son in years, the good is not found here.   48
For while the soul is bound in carnal bonds,
   confined within this prison's gloom, it will
   be always governed by desire and doubt.   51
The soul is so wrapped up in error when
   it's body-bound, that it won't know itself
   until its liberation is complete.   54
We see, therefore, that once it's severed from
   the flesh, the happy soul experiences
   the consummate attainment of this good.   57
So, to reward the virtuous, divine
   justice reserves, as I have said, this palm
   for those who dedicate themselves to God.   60

The things our soul may contemplate are two,
   angelic nature or divine. The first
   of these, however, brings no peace or rest: 63
our intellect, which Nature predisposes
   to seek the source of every thing that is,
   will ever run from one cause to the next,   66
and it will never reach repose or peace
   until it finds the root of every cause
   that's locked up in the mystery of God.   69
Our will, perforce, is always on the move—
   it's never sated by a good beyond
   which it perceives some new and greater joy.   72
It ever longs to reach the perfect good,
   and only finds repose in God's own light,
   when you have reached the sovereign good itself.   75
All things find rest in their own cause, and that
   is God; accordingly it's God, and not
   the Angels, who imparts this plenteous good.   78
Ispano, Al-Ghazal, and Avicenna
   esteemed the Angels as the highest good,
   but the true good is God the beautiful.   81
Yet there are two ways to reflect on God:
   in one we see Him through our intellect,
   and come to recognize Him by this means.   84
The second method is to know Him through
   desire and delight, and so achieve
   a joyous consummation of our longing.   87
The divine Plato, phoenix to our world,
   has named the first, the sight of God, "ambrosia."
   He calls the pleasure of this vision "nectar."   90
Our chaste and lovely soul, then, has two wings,
   desire and intellect, by which it rises,
   soaring to sovereign God, beyond the stars,   93
where it will dine on nectar and ambrosia
   at God's own feast; nor does this everlasting,
   immense, and sovereign sweetness ever fail.   96
More than ambrosia, nectar is the soul's
   delight, when it is sundered from the world,
   and pleasure satisfies it more than sight.   99

Since loving God in this life merits more
   than knowing Him, so in the life to come
   love's flower will procure the fruit of love.   102
I want to prove that love is worthier,
   and that the soul gets more in life by loving
   God's grace than by investigating it.   105
In the first place, so scant is human vision
   that no man gains true consciousness of God:
   in life is vision, rather, error's source.   108
But that man has a good and perfect will
   and loves God truly, who denies himself
   and all that he possesses for His sake.   111
Since he who hates God is more deeply wrong
   than he who fails to fathom Him at all,
   so he whose love is greater has more worth.   114
Nature and reason show the truth of this;
   to make my sense more firm and sure, I've based
   my proof upon the law of opposites.   117
Love opens up the gates of paradise:
   the loving soul will never err, whereas
   the search for knowledge often leads to death.   120
At times the pride of knowledge lifts one's spirit
   above the earth and veils the eyes: to one
   like that, God closes Himself off, and hides.   123
He hides from scholars, from the wise, but as
   the holy tongue itself once stated, Love
   reveals Him to the eyes of simple men.   126
He who sets out to analyze God's nature
   does Him no honor in this way—he does
   the work, perhaps, to glorify himself.   129
But he who grows enamored of His beauty,
   and gives himself and what he owns to God,
   to him will God present Himself in turn.   132
The soul that is intent on knowing God
   consumes much time without much gain—the soul
   that loves Him well is very soon content.   135
Thus, to conclude from all that has been said,
   if love is worthier, let no one think
   that love should not obtain the greater prize.   138

It's fitting, then, that those who seek to see
    should see, but lovers will enjoy their Love
    with infinite delight eternally.   141
Love is an ardent longing and desire.
    Love is what must obtain due recompense.
    Love is what makes the greater good appear,   144
as we will show with stronger evidence.

V

So full of sweetness was my heart while I
    was hearing him, I felt that I was pulled
    up to that Good of which his words did speak.   3
My soul, enraptured, drew apart. I wondered,
    "What, then, must truth itself be like, if I
    feel bliss when only hearing talk of it?"   6
Marsilio, having read my thoughts, then said
    to me, "By probing in yourself you'll sense
    which one of these two goods is whole and perfect.   9
You grasp my words, you're rather pleased. But once
    that pleasure's passed, the good you know awakes
    a newer, greater sweetness in your heart.   12
The mind, inflamed in its pursuit, now seeks
    possession of the good, but only to
    enjoy the good discerned: nor is it for   15
the sake of knowledge that it craves this pleasure.
    And so the understanding, which comes first,
    is servant to that good the mind desires.   18
To those who want to know what end it is
    we search for, we can answer: to enjoy
    the good that's first distinguished by our minds.   21
One can't give other grounds for joy than joy
    for its own sake, which never dies. Nor can
    the mind come into any greater good.   24
There is no pleasure human nature shuns,
    yet often we refuse to see what we
    consider troublesome or full of cares.   27

Who merely sees does not invariably
   rejoice at what he sees, but he whose mind
   feels joy will also see and understand. 30
And just as torment harms our nature more
   than lack of knowledge, so contrariwise
   does pleasure benefit us more than knowing. 33
No truthful judgment will diverge from ours:
   if suffering is the primal curse, then joy,
   its opposite, must be the final good. 36
Just as our nature flees from pain per se,
   and from whatever seems to lead to it,
   as from the very worst of punishments, 39
so too, the heart desires joy itself
   and all that's pleasurable, and runs to it
   as love will hasten to the sovereign good. 42
And just as one who only sees the good
   without desiring it, although he knows
   enough to choose the good, cannot be good, 45
so too, it's not just contemplating God
   but loving Him that makes our soul divine,
   for then the soul enjoys what first it knew. 48
When it's involved in knowing God, our soul
   must cut His vastness down to its own size,
   restricting Him within its narrow range. 51
But loving Him, we amplify the mind
   until it reaches His unbounded breadth.
   And this is what must be true happiness. 54
When seeing Him, we only grasp that bit
   of boundless might that is inside us, or
   that part the soul may see before its eyes. 57
When loving Him, you love both what you see
   and that more ample share of his immense
   benevolence the mind has promised you. 60
However long the soul intently stares
   we still will only see as through a fog
   the chasms of divine infinity. 63
We love Him with a true and perfect love:
   to know God is to drag Him down to earth;
   to love Him is to soar up to His height. 66

The sovereign good to which the mind aspires
  is happiness, but it won't find this if
  it merely meditates and looks on God,   69
because the vision that the seeing soul
  receives, however focused, always must
  be bound to something finite and created.   72
And so the soul may not desert its station:
  if as a force the soul is limited,
  its actions, too, are small and circumscribed.   75
But once it has escaped these bonds, the soul
  will only find complete content and rest
  in objects that possess eternal life.   78
The soul is only avid for the good
  that yields the God we cannot know. This longing
  and its fulfillment seem a boundless thing,   81
because, transmuted into God by love,
  the soul expands beyond that God whom we
  can only see." I broke my silence then   84
and said, "Now please explain this matter better,
  for it confounds my mind, no doubt because
  of some inherent blindspot in my heart."   87
Marsilio to me: "I'm not surprised
  some darkness compasses your soul—for that,
  however, you don't have to blame yourself.   90
No mortal eye can lift its gaze so high.
  To help your understanding, though, I'll use
  an illustration taken from the senses.   93
"Tasting" and "taste" are terms to be distinguished:
  the aptitude of savoring is "taste,"
  while "tasting" is the very act itself.   96
To set these two in motion one requires
  flavor—to serve them as a common object
  and cause the first to usher in the second.   99
Taste is the soul's desire, perfect, pure,
  aroused by tasting, which is intellect,
  to savor and enjoy the worthy object.   102
When it has reached this goal, the soul tastes God,
  enjoying Him with sacred lust, a joy
  whose flavor tastes of every other good.   105

The tasting gives us pleasure only when
   the flavor's sweet: the soul tastes God by seeing,
   but only passion gives it deep delight.   108
So we'll conclude, affirming that our true
   and sovereign good is that eternal God
   Whom we all unremittingly pursue,   111
that simple lamb, immaculate and pure,
   to whom our pilgrim soul now makes its way
   that it may rest within His blessed hostel.   114
The soul's most holy bliss is to enjoy
   this good by means of longing, for desire
   proceeds from love and leads the soul to God.   117
In Him the soul will taste that sweet delight
   for which, already, it has yearned so much,
   a sweetness no created thing can yield.   120
And when the soul loves God, it's apt that He
   invest it with His holy love, immerse
   our mind in His, and grant it endless joy.   123
Love is the just reward of love that's loved.
   Love is what gives us everlasting peace.
   Love is true health, unfailing and complete.   126
The blessed Apostle, witness to the truth,
   and vessel capable of so much grace,
   arrived as far as heaven through this love.   129
Love raised him to the third celestial realm,
   up to the star that fills the world with love,
   through which his eyes and God's became as one.   132
Within that sphere God never hides, but there
   reveals Himself, His holy domicile,
   His riches vast and inexhaustible.   135
For just above is that bright aperture
   which shows itself and everything that is,
   where only God has placed His tabernacle.   138
This prize is kept from us until our soul
   is sundered from the flesh; nor can my life
   or yours acquire it in this blind world.   141
But lives like ours within this world include
   so many evils that ferocious beasts
   inside some cave lead lives far happier.   144

The more the eyes of mortals see the good,
   the more they suffer from not having it:
     thus greater knowledge brings us greater woe.   147
Moreover, all the while we live our lives
   the sum of things we covet ever grows,
     yet beasts want only grass and cooling springs.   150
Who has the fewest needs is happiest:
   hence man appears least happy in this world,
     where all his life he dreams and vacillates.   153
But then the prize comes in his second life,
   that one the erring world calls 'gloomy death,'
     when he attains his bright and joyous end.   156
And so our life is not this worldly life
   (nor yours, oh shepherd, with its greater calm,
     nor Lauro is it yours, which seems so fair),   159
where not one moment of so many can
   be glad (this holds for every mortal life),
     for true delight will always spurn the world.   162
Since Phoebus seems to sink beneath the Ocean
   and with the setting sun my talk concludes,
     Adieu, Alfeo! Lauro, fare thee well!"   165
And so he left those lonely slopes, and us
   as well, who though beside a limpid spring,
     were thirsty still to hear his well-wrought speech,   168
whose words will never fade in Lethe's stream.
   But then the shepherd said, "It's late. I need
     to lead my modest flock back to its fold.   171
Already Phoebus's light abandons us,
   so I'll return to my old drudgery,
     and you, to where your inclinations lead."   174
This said, he put his flock in motion,
   whereupon I turned my back to him and, with
     a sluggish step, proceeded on my way.   177
So each went on to his own dwelling place,
   but as I glowed inside with sacred fire,
     and all my thoughts were sweetly wandering,   180
Love, who inflames all things, inspired me to sing.

VI

Oh venerable, immense, eternal Light,
  you who observe yourself within yourself.
  Oh light that shines through your divinity!   3
Oh boundless vision, which proceeds from you
  and through you glows, while every splendor shines
  through you by means of light that you bestow!   6
Oh spirit's eye, which only understands
  spiritual sight, and through which means this sight
  perceives and fathoms you and you alone.   9
Oh life immortal of each one who sees,
  oh perfect good of everyone who lives,
  which quenches every passion you inflame.   12
You kindle longing and the burning need
  to savor every good, for you alone
  are every good, oh you, our only hope.   15
Oh light resplendent, pure, and true, through you,
  I pray to you to cleanse my clouded vision
  of haze and make it absolutely clear   18
that I may see your pure and limpid light.
  For you ignite the thirst that's in my heart,
  you make my frozen heart catch fire and burn.   21
Expand the vision of my puny eye,
  so I can see you—elevate my downcast
  pupil, so it can see beyond the sky.   24
Allow your depth to penetrate and enter
  my inmost self, a depth that goes more deep,
  that's more profound than any other depth.   27
Let your sublimity, then, raise me up,
  sublimity of highest eminence
  and far surpassing every other virtue.   30
And may your marvelous, resplendent rays,
  of wondrous loveliness and goodness, pierce
  our souls, our flesh, and, most of all, our minds.   33
This grace, this goodness inexhaustible,
  allures me, warms, inflames, coerces me,
  unwitting me: oh rare lucidity!   36

Desire soars, but then the soul becomes
   lethargic, thinking that its finite passion
   can never merit everlasting glory.   39
Oh courage unexampled, high, supreme,
   may you extend your hand to my limp longing.
   Let your compassion heed my misery.   42
Unwavering hope, oh you my only refuge,
   direct the heart you call—receive, oh God,
   the one whom you compel to come to you.   45
Whom you afflict, give him delight and peace.
   Make cool the one you cause to burn. My hope
   is this, for you are perfect happiness.   48
The fount of every joy, of perfect bliss!
   I know that you're unique, and that in you
   resides whatever rouses our desire.   51
For if some good or other pleases us,
   our longing does not seek this good or that,
   but seeks the Good in them, where lies its peace. 54
The heart has sought the quality of Good
   in every thing, the healthful liquor living
   within itself and spreading through all else.   57
And to this water's fount the heart makes haste.
   It seeks and honors this perennial fount,
   which is diffused in every lowly thing.   60
Just as the only thing our eye perceives
   is sun, which shines in everything, so too
   is there one good alone the world desires.   63
Therefore, our thirst for this or that, or this
   and that together, never can be stilled
   until that other, greater good's revealed.   66
Only the fount that drips the sacred liquor
   allays and slakes our thirst: oh sacred liquor,
   allay this thirst that weighs upon me so.   69
Since no thing's good, except that you, oh Good
   of every good, invest it with your presence,
   don't let us be without you for so long.   72
Oh primal Mind, without forgetfulness,
   oh primal Wisdom, deep, sublime, profound,
   and never sullied by stupidity,   75

from whom there never is concealed one thing
  that your intelligence creates and orders
  through its abounding, endless providence.   78
You've not neglected even one of all
  the things your boundless love begets: in your
  perfection you watch over what's imperfect.   81
And yet your ardent love does everything—
  and this astounds my mind—to care for and
  to think of those who do not think of it.   84
Oh Grace abounding, oh compassionate Mind,
  how can it be that every slightest thing
  is fed and nourished and fulfilled by you,   87
but man, your marvelous creation, who
  adores and venerates your holy name
  is left to suffer such an avid thirst?   90
Man, I repeat, who honors you by faith
  alone. Release him from his endless worry,
  for he still hopes to rest in you alone.   93
May sad, injurious ingratitude
  flee from the boundless prodigality
  of your good deeds, of so much high renown.   96
And may deception flee from you, oh Truth,
  because the soul will certainly be deceived
  if after so much thirst it can't find joy.   99
So if for you it bears some heavy corpse,
  takes up its cross, and holds the world in scorn,
  you must reward it with the eternal palm.   102
Oh sovereign, ceaseless Good, prolific, vast!
  a man's more wretched than a stupid beast,
  if you refuse him joy within your country.   105
And yet your vase with every grace brims over.
  Therefore, I hope for that surcease of all my woes
  which owes more to your grace than to my merit.   108
And though our heart may mourn, this little while,
  its earthly sorrows, recompense us for
  these woes, these fleeting wants, with happiness,   111
with joy the passing years cannot allot.
  Instead of small and fleeting, give us great
  eternal good—you won't deceive us so.   114

Oh Savior who redeemed the world from hell,
   oh true retreat, who is the only health,
     you save each one who's subject to your rule.   117
Oh Good of goods, and Virtue of each virtue,
   I know you've given me eternal life
     so that I won't be baser than the beasts.   120
For your impassioned generosity
   instills in the mind's vessel love, through which
     we can become enamored of your goodness.   123
Likewise, our mind responds to yours, and if
   we understand, your mind illuminates
     for us those things that are sublime and deep.   126
As both our love and mind come from these two
   in you, so will the principle of your
     eternal life infuse our life as well.   129
We live, oh Life, for you. To us you give
   true cognizance of some immortal things,
     and over mortal things, the will to rule.   132
First, you awakened life in us, eternal
   in its response to yours, eternal, changeless,
     and placed in us before desire or mind.   135
So with these three, each soul in its own way
   is able to enjoy eternity,
     is made immortal, made to last forever: 138
the mind, through finding out; the righteous will,
   through longing; and above all else, the life
     we live that's granted us and never dies.   141
Eternity informs the mind and will,
   which follow life; and thus, before all else,
     it enters life, which is created first.   144
You will, then, put an end to my distress.
   Through grace abounding, through the law of our
     inheritance, our hearts will compass bliss.   147
Give us right now, at least some share of this.
   Let us enjoy, a little in this life,
     the certain hope of your benevolence.   150
If you're unwilling still, because our soul
   is undeserving still, at least, we beg,
     show us the open way to our salvation.   153

Grant us that you won't let us be deceived
   by brief terrestrial allures, or lose
   what's sure for what is vain and insecure.   156
While strengthening our heart against the rule
   of dreadful Fortune and her threat, to which,
   sometimes, the man who's so inclined succumbs,   159
show us the kindness of your holy face.
   Oh Father most indulgent with your sons,
   May your compassion open wide its arms.   162
Oh ample Good, *recrea quos creasti.*
   Help us, for we are born of you alone,
   almighty Father and most merciful.   165
Only your truth and goodness consummate
   and slake our thirsty minds and wills, nor do
   we understand the Cause that fashioned us.   168
Have pity on your sick, infected child,
   the soul, so far from her celestial homeland,
   who's banished to this dark and murky woods.   171
Lift from our heart whatever keeps you distant.
   Have pity on the grievous longing for
   our native land, which pierces through our heart.   174
There, where our homeland is, dwells true repose.
   Where home and father are, the son will rest.
   There dwells the highest good, abundant, true.   177
In exile there is worry and false good,
   or rather real and flagrant wickedness.
   Admit us, then, to your divine assembly.   180
If, then, some good is offered to the heart,
   we then will live removed from wicked thoughts.
   The soul will taste a good that is assured   183
when our devout and willing hearts reflect
   on you. The soul, it seems, attains its good
   if it directs each of its prayers to you.   186
And should its thought unite with you, it then
   will rest. So rid us of whatever may
   distract the soul from thinking such a thought.   189
Release us from our doubt, our coldness, our
   despair, and let the soul take refuge, then,
   in faith and hope and loving charity,   192

so that we'll never be divorced from you,
   oh Life of lives, true Light, the only one
   who can illumine every other light.   195
Without your divine power, guided by
   our wits alone, we'll stray from the true path
   and rapidly fall into outer darkness.   198
Induce our soul, from birth until its term,
   to live for you alone—to shine within
   your light, when it has passed the final threshold.   201
May it blaze with joy in you, for it is led
   to you, unbounded Goodness, Truth, and Life,
   through you, the Way, who guides us to this good.   204
And make us love your boundless beauty, free
   of any care that might the heart torment.
   Oh sovereign Good, inciting every mind,   207
   let us enjoy you always, avid yet content.

The Supreme Good

The first version of this long, philosophical poem was composed in 1473–74 and then, according to Martelli 1965a, 1–35, expanded and revised in subsequent years. The work is a primary document for understanding a major turning point in Lorenzo's life, toward Neoplatonism and the spiritual concerns of his mentor Marsilio Ficino. Like the "Symposium," the poem was influenced by Dante's *Comedy*, but here the tone is serious and didactic rather than comic and satiric. Although capitoli 1 and 2 (to line 108) are Lorenzo's original creation, the other capitoli are largely a verse translation of two letters of Ficino, one on happiness (*De felicitate*) and the other a prayer to God (*Oratio ad Deum theologica*, the basis for capitolo 6). Lorenzo's original contribution is a lively dispute (*altercazione*) between him, Lauro, and Alfeo, the shepherd, about whether city or country life is more conducive to happiness. Alfeo, though not denying the corruptness of the city, points out to Lauro the bitter hardships of rustic life, thereby subverting Lauro's rosy view of pastoral existence. Enter Marsilio, who, Neoplatonically, proceeds to separate the question of happiness or the true good from the material conditions of life. After a long, subtle discourse Marsilio shows the inferiority of various kinds of good and proves that the loving contemplation of God is the only satisfying good: love rather than knowledge of God is the way to happiness. Lauro is then inspired to sing his hymn of praise to God. Though Lorenzo follows Ficino's prose fairly closely, he does, in the words of Martelli, invest Ficino's graceful text with a "surprising dramatic intensity" (1965a, 29). Likewise the hymn to God is both more passionate and more soul-searching that the Ficinian original (Sturm 125).

On the debate over the priority and relations of the Ficinian and Laurentian texts, see Wadsworth, Rochon 475–543, Kristeller, Martelli 1965a, 1–35, Orvieto 1976, 27–37, and Fubini in *Lettere* 1, 496–99, 510–11. For the background to the love-versus-intellect debate that lies behind Ficino's letter on happiness and capitoli 4 and 5, see Michael J. B. Allen, *Marsilio Ficino: The Philebus Commentary* (Berkeley and Los Angeles: University of California Press, 1975) 35–48. On the influence of capitoli 1 and 2 on Sannazaro's *Arcadia*, see Orvieto 1976, 33. I have followed the standard text in Bigi 1965 but have translated the other title, "De summo bono," rather than "Altercazione." Chastel's French and Stange's German translations were occasionally helpful in interpreting the text.

I.11–12.	*that mountain*, etc.: Mount Giovi, near Lorenzo's villa at Careggi, meeting place of the Platonic Academy, led by Ficino; the mountain is old and so is its name, Giovi (with a wordplay on youth), which goes back to its youth.
II.5.	*or he whose noble tones had walled up Thebes*: Amphion, the mythical lyre player and King of Thebes, whose sweet music caused the stones to move of their own accord and make themselves into walls.
II.7.	*that lyre*: the lyre of Orpheus, which became, after his death, a constellation.
II.10.	*that ancient sage*: Pythagoras, who believed in the transmigration of souls (reincarnation).
II.19.	*Marsilio of Montevecchio*: Marsilio Ficino, whose Platonic Academy sometimes met near Montevecchio.
II.100–102.	*But drawing out this point*, etc.: in other words, I do not want to turn you off by overdoing this analogy (seeking the good too soon/eating unripe fruit), an analogy that might have the same effect as the mildly ridiculous one comparing heaven (the sky) to a stretched-out pelt.

II.109.   At this point Lorenzo begins to use Ficino's letter on happiness. See Ficino 1985, vol. 1, Letter 115.

II.148.   *And he who took goodwill*: Augustus Caesar.

III.2.   *the newborn Plato*: that is, Marsilio, translator of Plato into Latin.

III.8.   *Milo*: renowned athlete of ancient Greece.

III.13.   *Herillus*: a Carthaginian philosopher.

III.34.   *Aristippus*: ancient Greek philosopher and student of Socrates.

III.82–83.   *Zeno . . . the Cynic rabble*: Zeno (c. 300 B.C.) was the founder of Stoic philosophy. He, along with the Cynics, maintained that the exercise of the active virtues was the highest good.

III.103–5.   Lorenzo follows here the traditional identification of Mary Magdalen with the contemplative life, favored by Jesus, and Martha with the active life. See the Gospel of Luke 10.38–42.

III.111–12.   Cf. the Gospel of John 4.7–15, where the water that prevents the return of thirst is identified with the teachings of Jesus.

III.124.   *Democritus*: ancient Greek philosopher (born c. 460 B.C.).

III.134.   *Anaxagoras*: ancient Greek philosopher who lived in the fifth century B.C.

IV.19.   *the mighty Thunderer's daughter*: Minerva, who was born from Jupiter's head, and thus represents, in Ficinian thought, the contemplative life. Lorenzo now abandons Pan, the more worldly god (4.3–6), as his inspiration and calls on Minerva to help him sing the higher mysteries of contemplation.

IV.37–38.   *Apollo . . . your much-desired Daphne*: Apollo chased the nymph Daphne, who was saved by being changed into a laurel tree. Lorenzo is Lauro, and Lauro is the laurel tree.

IV.79.   *Ispano, Al-Ghazal, and Avicenna*: medieval Arab philosophers. Ispano is Averroes (1126–98).

IV.88.   *The divine Plato, phoenix to our world*: Plato is like a phoenix because of his uniqueness (Bigi 1965, 72).

IV.82.   The rest of Marsilio's discourse concerns the much-discussed question of whether the will or the intellect is the better means of approaching God. See Allen 1975, 35–48, for the historical roots of this controversy.

V.1–93. In this section Lorenzo's poetic expression of Ficino's thought is at its most inspired and compelling.

V.93–108. *an illustration taken from the senses*, etc.: far from helping the reader's understanding, this confused and confusing analogy does the opposite.

V.124–65. In this section Lorenzo ceases to paraphrase Ficino's letter but elaborates through his own vivid images the Ficinian theme of the will's and love's superiority to intellect.

V.127. *The blessed Apostle*: Saint Paul, who wrote of having been transported to heaven, see 2 Corinthians 12.1–4.

V.130. *the third celestial realm*: that is, the planet Venus.

V.136–38. *that bright aperture*, etc.: the sense, if not the imagery, of these lines is not easy to understand: *the bright aperture* may be God himself, as in Dante's vision in the *Paradiso* 28.13–21, 29.12, 33.87, and/or an *aleph* or magical point that contains all other points in the cosmos and makes them visible, also a characteristic of Dante's God.

VI.1–208. This prayer to God is an inspired translation of Ficino's *Oratio ad Deum theologica*.

VI.163. *recrea quos creasti*: revive those whom you have created.

Sonnets

1. (XXIX)

I saw my Lady by a purling brook
    With laughing maidens, where green branches twined;
    O never since that primal, passionate look
    Have I beheld her face so soft and kind.
Hence for a space my yearning was content
    And my sad soul some consolation knew;
    Alas, my heart remained although I went,
    And constantly my pain and sorrow grew.
Early the sun sank down in western skies
    And left the earth to woeful hours obscure,
    Afar my sun hath also veiled her ray;
Upon the mind first bliss most heavily lies,
    How short a while all mortal joys endure,
    But not so soon doth memory pass away.

Translated by Lorna De' Lucchi

2. (XLVIII)

How every hope of ours is raised in vain,
    How spoiled the plans we laid so fair and well,
    How ignorance throughout the earth doth reign,
    Death, who is mistress of us all, can tell.
In song and dance and jousts some pass their days,
    Some vow their talents unto gentle arts,
    Some hold the world in scorn and all its ways,
    Some hide the impulses that move their hearts.

Vain thoughts and wishes, cares of every kind
   Greatly upon this erring earth prevail
   In various presence after nature's lore;
Fortune doth fashion with inconstant mind,
   All things are transient here below and frail,
   Death only standeth fast for evermore.

Translated by Lorna De' Lucchi

3. (LIV)

Leave your beloved isle, you Cyprian queen;
   Leave your enchanted realm so delicate,
   Goddess of love! Come where the rivulet
   Bathes the short turf and blades of tenderest green!
Come to these shades, these airs that stir the screen
   Of whispering branches and their murmurs set
   To the love bird's enamoured canzonet:
   Choose this for your own land, your loved domain!
And if you come by these clear rills to reign,
   Bring your dear son, your darling progeny;
   For there be none that knows his empire here.
From Dian steal the vestals of her train,
   Who roam the woods at will, from danger free,
   And know not Love, nor his dread power fear.

Translated by John Addington Symonds

4. (LVIII)
Sonnet made for the Duke of Calabria
in the name of a woman

"Enough to have robbed me of my liberty,
   Turned me from path of virtue and misled,
   Without desiring to see me dead
   At age so tender and so cruelly.

All without pity you abandoned me;
   And in my pale and wan face might be read
   True presage of a life to be quick sped;
   And now I care not I am fair to see.
Nor can I think of aught else than that hour
   Which was occasion of my tender sighs,
   Of my sweet martyrdom and woeful gain;
And had not fond remembrance still the power
   Unhappy lovers' hearts to tranquillize,
   Death would have put an end to so great pain."

Translated by Jefferson Butler Fletcher

5. (LXXXIV)

Not from the verdant garden's cultured bound,
   That breathes of Paestum's aromatic gale,
   We sprung; but nurslings of the lonely vale,
   'Midst woods obscure, and native glooms were found:
'Midst woods and glooms, whose tangled brakes around
   Once Venus sorrowing traced, as all forlorn
   She sought Adonis, when a lurking thorn
   Deep on her foot impress'd an impious wound.
Then prone to earth we bow'd our pallid flowers,
   And caught the drops divine; the purple dyes
   Tinging the lustre of our native hue:
Nor summer gales, nor art-conducted showers
   Have nursed our slender forms, but lovers' sighs
   Have been our gales, and lovers' tears our dew.

Translated by William Roscoe

6. (CII)

Ah pearly drops, that pouring from those eyes,
   Spoke the dissolving cloud of soft desire!

What time cold sorrow chill'd the genial fire,
    "Struck the fair urns and bade the waters rise."
Soft down those cheeks, where native crimson vies
    With ivory whiteness, see the crystals throng;
    As some clear river winds its stream along,
    Bathing the flowers of pale and purple dyes.
Whilst Love, rejoicing in the amorous shower,
    Stands like some bird, that after sultry heats
    Enjoys the drops, and shakes his glittering wings;
Then grasps his bolt, and conscious of his power,
    'Midst those bright orbs assumes his wonted seat,
    And thro' the lucid shower his living lightning flings.

Translated by William Roscoe

Sonnets

All the sonnets are from the Canzoniere (the roman numerals refer to Orvieto's numbering system, 1984). Few of Lorenzo's sonnets have been translated, and fewer still have been translated well, hence this very limited selection (see also the Introduction). These versions reflect styles of translation from three centuries, with Roscoe representing the eighteenth, Symonds the nineteenth, and Fletcher and De' Lucchi the twentieth. My glosses are indebted to the excellent commentaries in Orvieto 1984.

1. (XXIX): A Petrarchan sonnet on the absence of the beloved, probably Lucrezia Donati.

2. (XLVIII): The topos of the vanity of worldly pursuits echoes capitolo 1 of "The Supreme Good."

3. (LIV): The Cyprian Queen is Venus, who dwells on the isle of Cyprus. Your dear son is Love or Cupid. From Dian steal . . . , that is, make the chaste nymphs of Diana know love. I have made some minor revisions in Symonds's translation.

4. (LVIII): This sonnet is probably an allegory: the woman is Florence; the lover is the Duke of Calabria, who visited Florence for a year (1467–68). Thus the Duke "seduced" Florence, and when he left the city, he "abandoned" her. The lament of the abandoned woman was a conventional form.

5. (LXXXIV): This lovely sonnet probably accompanied a bouquet of roses sent to the author's beloved. Roscoe's translation is rather free. The conceit is based on a classical myth: Venus in pursuit of her lover, Adonis, pricks her foot on a rose thorn, roses then being white. The roses prevent her sacred blood from falling on the ground, but in doing so are stained red. *Paestum* was an ancient Greek city in Italy famed for its roses. *We sprung*, i.e., we, the roses.

6. (CII): Roscoe's translation is very free. The sense is as follows: the *cold sorrow* distills the *cloud of desire* in the heart (*the genial fire*), causing tears to rise in the lady's eyes (*fair urns*). In the second quatrain, the tears on the ivory and crimson cheeks resemble a river watering *pale* and *purple flowers*. Then in the tercets, Cupid or Love bathes in the *shower*, and next he enters the eyes (*those bright orbs*), where the glint of tears becomes the *living lightning* he flings out. Her tears, in other words, excite the lover's passion. Water paradoxically engenders fire.

A Commentary on My Sonnets
(the prologue and the first commentary)

Translated by Murray Linwood Marshall and Jon Thiem

I have been greatly in doubt as to whether I should make this interpreta-
tion of, and commentary on, my sonnets. And if indeed I have at times
been inclined to make it, the following reasons have deterred and dis-
suaded me from undertaking this work. First of all, there is the charge of
presumption that, it seemed to me, I would incur by commenting upon my
own writings, as much from the too high estimate I appeared to make of
myself, as because I seemed to arrogate to myself the judgment that right-
fully belongs to others, thus suggesting that the minds of those in whose
hands my verses would come were little capable of understanding them. I
have also thought that someone might easily reprove me for poor judg-
ment, for having spent my time composing and commenting on verses
whose subject matter was in large part the passion of love. This might be
considered most reprehensible in me because of the ever-present respon-
sibilities, both public and private, that should draw me away from such
thoughts—thoughts that are, according to some people, not only frivolous
and of little moment, but also pernicious and prejudicial both to our soul
and to our worldly honor. If this is true, thinking about such things is a
great error; putting them into verse is a much greater one; but commenting
on them does not seem less of a failing than that of a person who has had
a long and hardened habit of doing evil deeds, this being all the more true
since commentaries are usually reserved for theological and philosophical
matters, and lead to momentous conclusions, or to the edification and
consolation of the soul, or to the use and benefit of humanity. In addition,
there is this reason: even though the subject matter may be worthy
enough, to some it will perhaps seem reprehensible that I have written and
made mention of these things in the vernacular, our mother tongue, which,
because it is so common where it is spoken and understood, will seem
somehow lowly and despicable. And in those places where there is no
knowledge of this tongue, it will not be understood: therefore, in these

places this commentary and my efforts will seem to have been all in vain, as if it had never been done at all.

These three difficulties have delayed until now what I some time ago had planned, namely, the present interpretation. Now, however, having been won over by what are in my view better reasons, I have made up my mind to go ahead with this interpretation, believing that, if this small labor of mine merits the esteem or gratitude of some one person, it will have been well employed and not wholly in vain. If, however, it is badly received, it will be read by few and by few reviled. And, not being very long-lived, it will suffer little enough from the censure it may incur.

So, in answer now to the first objection and to those people who would in some way or another charge me with presumption, I say that it seems to me that the interpretation of my own writings is not so much presumption as the elimination of the work that others would otherwise have to do. Nor is the task of interpretation more appropriate for anyone than for the author himself, because no one else is better able to know or truly determine what he means, as is shown clearly enough by the confusion that arises from the variety of commentaries, in which the commentators usually follow their own inclination rather than the true intention of the author. Nor does this argument mean, it seems to me, that I rate myself too highly or that I deprive others of the right to judge me, for I believe that it is the fundamental duty of every man to work in all things for the benefit of mankind, whether for his own or others' benefit. And since not everyone is born capable of achieving those things that are judged as first in the world, each person should measure himself, determine the occupation in which he is best able to serve humanity, and exercise himself in that capacity, for no one occupation can satisfy both the wide diversity of human talents and the necessities of human life, even if it were the highest and most excellent work that men can do. Not even contemplation, it seems, which is indisputably the highest and most [. . .][1] And from this, one concludes that not only many works of genius but also many lowly occupations necessarily contribute to the perfection of human life, and that it is the fundamental duty of all men to serve humanity in whatever capacity heaven, nature, or fortune has allotted them. I would have been well pleased to be able to undertake greater tasks. Yet I do not wish, even at a level that sustains my talent and powers, to fail one particular person[2] and perhaps many more whose authority and goodwill I greatly value, who have encouraged me in this task, more perhaps because they would please me than because my efforts satisfy them. And, if I cannot be of any other use to those who will read my verses, may readers at least derive some small pleasure from them, for perhaps they will find some ability proportionate and conforming to their own. Even if someone should laugh at these verses, it will please me that he can extract from them this pleasure, however small it is, and it will be all the more pleasing to me, I feel, since by publishing this interpretation I have willingly submitted myself to the judgment of others. This is because if I myself had judged these verses of mine as unworthy of being read, I would have fled the judgment of others. But by commenting on and publishing them, I think I am much better able to avoid the accusation of presumption for having judged myself by myself alone.

Now, in reply to the calumnies of those who might accuse me of having used my time in composing and commenting on things not worth the time or effort because they concern amorous passions, especially when I have many unavoidable responsibilities, I say that I really should be condemned, and with justice, if human nature were endowed with such excellence that all men might always be able to do all things perfectly. But, because this degree of perfection has been conceded to very few and since these few achieve it even more rarely in their lives, it seems to me possible to conclude that, given human perfection, those things in the world are best through which the least evil comes.

And judging, moreover, from the common nature and universal habits of men, I do believe, though I dare not affirm it, that love among men is not only not reprehensible, but is virtually necessary, and that it is a very sure sign of gentilezza[3] and greatness of soul, and that, above all, it draws men to worthy and excellent things and to exercising and translating into action those virtues that exist in a potential state in our souls. For he who searches diligently for the true definition of love finds that it is none other than the desire for beauty. If this is so, then all deformed and ugly things will necessarily displease the one who loves.

Putting aside for the present that love through which, according to Plato, all things attain their perfection and ultimately rest in the supreme Beauty, which is God, I will speak exclusively of the love that extends only to loving the human creature. I say that even if this creature is not the perfection of love that is called the "supreme good,"[4] at least we clearly see that it contains many goods and shuns many evils, and that, according to the common practice of human life, it takes the part of the good, especially if it is endowed with those circumstances and conditions that are necessary to a true love. These, it seems to me, are two: the first is that one love one

thing alone; the second, that one love this thing always.[5] These two condi-
tions can hardly be fulfilled unless the loved object possesses, in compari-
son to other human beings, the highest perfection, and unless, besides the
properties of natural beauty, there converge in the loved object great intel-
ligence, graceful habits, an elegant manner and gestures, sagacity, discern-
ment, tender words, love, constancy, and faith. All of these qualities are
necessary and appropriate to the perfection of love, because, even though
love originates by way of the eyes and beauty, nevertheless for the preser-
vation and persistence of love these other attributes are essential. For if,
either through infirmity or age or some other cause, the face should be-
come sallow and lose, in whole or part, its beauty, all these other attri-
butes would remain not less pleasing to the mind and heart than beauty to
the eyes. Nor would even these attributes suffice, if there were not also in
the one who loves a true knowledge of these attributes, which presupposes
perfection of judgment on the lover's part. Nor can the thing loved love
the one who loves if the latter does not deserve being loved, which presup-
poses unerring judgment on the part of the thing loved.

Therefore, he who proposes a true love, of necessity proposes great per-
fection, according to the common usage of men, both in the loved one and
in the lover. And, as is true of all other perfect things, such a love as this
has, I believe, existed very seldom in the world, which argues all the more
for its excellence. He who loves one thing only and that always, of neces-
sity does not extend his love to other things. As a result he avoids all of the
errors and sensual pleasures into which men commonly fall, and by loving
an intelligent person and by seeking in every way possible to please that
person, he must necessarily endeavor to make himself worthy in all his
actions, and make himself excel among the others, pursuing virtuous ac-
tions in order to make himself as worthy as possible to the one whom he
judges worthy above all the others. And just as it seems to him that the
form of the loved one is always present to his heart, whether she is actually
there or not, so too is she present in all his actions, praising or reproving
them for their suitability, as a true witness and ever-present judge, not only
of his deeds but also his thoughts. And so, partly by repressing wickedness
out of a feeling of shame, and partly by engendering goodness through the
urge to please the loved one, such lovers as these, even if their actions are
not perfect, at least do that which is reputed in the world to be less evil,
and this is the course one does best to choose, given the imperfections of
human beings in this world.

This then has been the subject of my verses, and if all these arguments will not answer the accusations and calumnies of those who would condemn me, at least, as our Florentine poet has said, concerning those who know through experience what love is, "I hope to find pity, not only pardon."[6] The judgment of these is enough to satisfy me. For, if it is true, as Guido of Bologna says, that love and gentilezza are interchangeable and one and the same thing, then I believe that men will be satisfied with the praise of high and noble minds, finding it alone desirable, and that they will pay little heed to other minds, since it is impossible to do anything in the world that will be praised by all men. Therefore, he who has true discernment will try to acquire praise from those who likewise are worthy of praise and who pay little heed to the opinions of others. It seems to me that one can little blame that which is natural; and nothing is more natural than the desire to unite oneself with a beautiful object. This desire has been placed by nature in men for the purpose of human propagation, which is necessary for the preservation of the human species. Hence the real motive that should impel us is not nobility of blood and not the hope of acquiring wealth, possessions, or other sources of ease, but only natural choice that is not forced or swayed by any other consideration, but that is moved solely by a certain conformity and proportion shared by the loved one and the lover for the purpose of propagating the human species. Therefore those people should be most condemned whom desire moves to love most intensely things that are outside of this natural order and beyond the true goal already proposed by us, while those people should be most praised who, pursuing this goal, love one thing alone continuously and with firm constancy and faith.

It seems to me that I have responded very fully to this objection concerning my subject. Granted then, that this love, as we have said above, is good, it does not seem very necessary to vindicate that part of me which might seem more than reprehensible because of my various public and private responsibilities. For, if it is good, the good has no need of any justification, since there is no wrongdoing. Yet even if some scrupulous judge might not want to accept these arguments, may he concede at least this small license to tender, youthful age, which does not seem as subject to the censure and judgment of men. It is an age in which no error seems so very serious, especially because youth is more impelled, on account of little experience, to leave the straight and narrow way, and is less able to resist those things to which it is won over by nature and the common practice of others. I say this in case it might be judged an error to love deeply, with the greatest sincerity and faith, an object that, because of its perfection, compels the love of the lover. Nor do I acknowledge that this is an error. And if it is not, either for the reasons stated above or for the indulgence due to youthful age, neither the composing nor the exposition of my verses, written with this purpose in mind,[7] can be imputed to me as a grave error. And assuming that it might be true that it is not appropriate for me to comment on such material because it is small in quantity and of little importance either for the edification or contentment of the mind, still I say that if this is true, the labor of writing this commentary is especially appropriate for me in order that another mind of greater excellence than mine may not have to consume itself or waste time on things so lowly. And yet if the subject is lofty and worthwhile, as I think it is, to explain it properly and to make it plain and intelligible to everyone is very useful. And for the two reasons stated above, no one is able to do this with a clearer expression of the real meaning than I myself. Nor am I the first to have commented on verses that contain similar amorous themes, for Dante himself commented on some of his canzoni and other verses. I have also read Egidio Romano and Dino del Garbo, most excellent philosophers, on that very subtle canzone of Guido Cavalcanti, a man reputed in his time to be the greatest dialectician in the world, whose excellence is revealed not only in these excellent vernacular verses but also in all his other works and especially in the above-mentioned canzone, which begins "Woman begs me," etc., and treats of nothing else than the principle whereby love is born in gentle hearts, and its effects.[8] If, however, neither the above-written arguments nor these precedents are enough to exonerate me, at least compassion should absolve me of guilt, because, having been in my youth much persecuted by men and by fortune,[9] I should not be denied some little solace, which I have found solely in loving fervently and in composing and commenting on my verses, as I will explain more clearly when we come to the exposition of that sonnet which begins "If in the midst of other sighs that issue forth" etc. It is impossible that anyone but I could comprehend how malicious the persecutions inflicted on me have been, for all that they have been done openly and have been well publicized, or how sweet a solace my most tender and constant love has been in the face of these persecutions. For even if I had told these things to someone, it would have been as impossible for him to understand them as for me to communicate their truth. Therefore, I come back to the above-mentioned verse of our Florentine poet, for among those who through experience understand love (both the love that I have praised so much and any particular love and charity toward myself), "I hope to find pity, not only pardon."

Now there only remains for me to reply to the objection that might be made because of my having written in the vulgar tongue, which, according to the judgment of some, is incapable and unworthy of giving utterance to any subject of excellence.

To this argument one may reply that no thing is less worthy for being more common. On the contrary, it is evident that every good is so much the better, the more it is communicable and universal, as is by its very nature that which we call the "supreme good." For it would not be supreme if it were not infinite, nor can anything be called infinite if it is not common to all things.

Therefore, it does not seem that being common to all Italy will rob our mother tongue of its dignity. One does need to ponder, however, the issue of whether or not this language possesses perfection. After some consideration, it seems to me that those conditions that give dignity and perfection to any dialect or language are four in number. Of these four, one or at the most two are intrinsic merits of the language itself, whereas the other conditions depend rather on the customs and opinions of men or on fortune. One truly intrinsic merit of the language itself is the copiousness and richness of its vocabulary and its ability to express well the mind's ideas and sense. Thus the Greek tongue is considered more perfect than the Latin and the Latin more than the Hebrew, because the one, more than the other, better expresses the mind of the speaker or the writer. Another condition that gives one language more dignity than another is its sweetness and harmony. Although harmony is both a natural phenomenon and commensurate with the harmony of our souls and bodies, even so, it seems to me that because of the variety of human minds, not all of which are perfect and well proportioned, the discernment of harmony is more often based on opinion than reason. This is because those things that are judged according to whether they are usually pleasing or not are so judged, it seems, more on the basis of opinion than of sound reasoning, and this is especially true of things whose capacity or incapacity to give pleasure is established through no other rationale than desire. Yet in spite of these reasons I do not want to affirm that harmony cannot be an intrinsic merit of the language itself, for insofar as harmony is, as I said, commensurate with human nature, one can infer that the discernment of its sweetness is the endowment of those who, like harmony itself, are well proportioned and so able to receive it. Their discernment should be accepted as just, even though they may be few in number, for one should ponder, rather than count, the judgments and insights of men.

Another condition that makes a language superior occurs when that language possesses writings containing subtle, weighty matters and things necessary to human life, necessary, that is, to our minds, to the body's health, and to the general benefit of men. One can say this of the Hebrew language because it contains wonderful mysteries that are well suited, even necessary, to the infallible truth of our faith. So too the Greek language, which contains many branches of learning—metaphysical, scientific, and moral—that are very necessary to humanity. But when this condition occurs, it must be admitted that the subject matter is more deserving of praise than the tongue itself, for the subject matter is the end and the tongue only the means. Nor from this can one say that a tongue is more perfect in itself, only that the subject matter that it treats is more perfect. Thus those who have written on theological, metaphysical, scientific, and moral matters, when they consider the merits of the tongue in which they have written, seem to reserve their praise more for the subject matter, and to use the tongue as a tool, which is good or bad according to the end it serves.

There remains only one other condition that gives a language great renown, and this occurs when the development of world events is such that these render universal and nearly popular throughout the world a tongue that belongs naturally to one city or province alone. One can more readily call this a happy success due to fortune than a real merit of the language itself, for the high estimation and worldly fame of a language depends on the opinion of those who greatly esteem and prize it. Nor can one call that which depends on others, rather than itself, a real and intrinsic good, because precisely those who value a language, might easily change their minds and scorn it. Or with a change in historical circumstances and the disappearance of the cause of esteem, the value and fame of the language would also easily disappear. The sort of worth that results from fortunate circumstances is very pertinent to the Latin language, for the spread of the Roman empire made it not only common but almost necessary to the whole world. So from this we can conclude that such external merits, and those that depend on the opinion of others or on fortune, are not intrinsic merits of the language itself.

Therefore, if we want to demonstrate the worth of our language, we need only insist upon the first condition: that our language easily expresses any concept our minds may have. For this, no better argument can be introduced than that from experience.

Our Florentine poets, Dante, Petrarch, and Boccaccio, have in their grave and very mellifluous verses and orations shown very clearly and with great facility their ability to express in our language every nuance of meaning. For he who reads Dante's *Commedia* will find there many theological and scientific subjects that are expressed with great adeptness and ease. He will also find very aptly represented in his writing those three kinds of style praised by orators, namely, the low, middle, and high styles. Indeed Dante, all by himself, has taken up and perfected with consummate artistry that which is found in various authors, both Latin and Greek. Who will deny that we find in Petrarch a style by turns grave, festive, and sweet, or that he treats this subject of love with a profundity and charm that certainly cannot be found in Ovid, Tibullus, Catullus, Propertius, or any other Latin writer? The canzoni and sonnets of Dante are of such gravity, subtlety, and elegance that they have virtually no equal in prose or oratory. He who has read Boccaccio, a man of great learning and facility of expression, will find it easy to rate not only his originality, but also his copiousness and eloquence, as singular and unique in the world. And if he considers his work, the *Decameron*, and what it contains, with its variety of subject matter, now sublime, now humble, now in the middle range, with all the perturbations that men undergo as a result of love, hate, fear, and hope, with so many new wiles and crafty contrivances, and with all the types and passions of men that are found in the world, he will conclude hands down that no language is better than ours for apt and flexible expression. And concerning Guido Cavalcanti, whom I mentioned before, it is impossible to describe how felicitously he has conjoined gravity with sweetness, as is shown by the canzone mentioned above and by some of his very charming sonnets and ballads.

There are also many other serious and elegant writers, the mention of whom I will omit rather to avoid prolixity than because they are undeserving. Therefore, I will conclude that there is rather a deficiency of men to exploit the language than a deficiency of language available to men and their subject matter. The sweetness and harmony of this tongue, to those who have become accustomed to it and who to some extent habitually employ it, are truly very great and well suited to move many people.

These, then, which are, and which may even seem to some other people to be, the intrinsic merits of a language, seem to me to be sufficiently abundant in our tongue. Considering especially what Dante has up to now treated in his works, I think that it is not only useful but also necessary for the profound effects that they convey, that his verses be read. This is demonstrated by the example of the many commentaries on his *Commedia* made by very learned and renowned men, and by the frequent quotations that one hears every day in the public sermons of eminent holy men. And perhaps more works that are subtle, important, and worthy to be read will yet be written in this language, especially since up to now the language has been, one can say, in its adolescence, for it continually grows more noble and elegant. And it could easily achieve in youth or adulthood still greater perfection, all the more so if in addition there should occur some fortunate political circumstance and an increase in Florentine power, for which one should not only hope but for which all good citizens should strive with all of their strength and intelligence. And yet, since such things depend on the sway of Fortune and the will and infallible judgment of God, it is better not to assert they will happen. Nor yet should one despair of them. It is enough for the present to draw this conclusion: that our tongue is richly endowed with those merits that are intrinsic to a language, so there is no justification for complaining about it. And for these same reasons no one can reproach me because I have written in the language in which I was born and nourished, especially since Hebrew, Greek, and Latin were all in their time natural mother tongues. The difference is that these languages were spoken and written more accurately (following some basic rules) by those held in high esteem than by the common people, as a rule.

It seems to have been proven with sufficient enough reasons that our language is inferior to no other. Therefore, having demonstrated its perfection on a general level, I think it very appropriate now to restrict myself to the consideration of particulars, and to move from generalities to some specific attributes, as one moves from circumference to center.

And so, since my purpose is to interpret my sonnets, I will try to show that among the verse forms usually available to those who have written in Italian, the style of the sonnet is not inferior to terza rima, the canzone, or other vernacular genres. I will base my argument on the difficulty of composing the sonnet, for *virtù*, according to the philosophers, entails that which is difficult.[10]

It is a saying of Plato's that for a person to tell many things briefly and lucidly seems not only marvelous among men, but almost a divine thing. The brevity of the sonnet does not tolerate the addition of a single useless word. And for this reason the real subject matter of a sonnet should be some pithy, exalted idea, aptly expressed in a few concise verses that avoid obscurity and harshness. This manner of composition is very similar to that of the epigram, especially with regard to the perspicacity of the material and the adroitness of the style, but the sonnet is both worthy and capable of conveying more serious ideas, and for this reason it is all the more difficult. I admit that terza rima involves a grander, more elevated style and that it is nearly equivalent to the heroic style.[11] Nevertheless, it is not any more difficult, for its range is wider, and with terza rima a writer can elaborate the kind of idea that could not be squeezed into two or three verses without the commission of a serious mistake. The canzone or song seems to me to be very similar to the elegy. But I think that this is due either to our particular way of writing in the vernacular or to the habitual practice of those who have written canzoni up to now, for the style of the canzone, not without some little touch of shame, encompasses many subjects that are not only vain and frivolous but also are excessively soft and lascivious, such as those commonly found in Latin elegies.[12] Moreover, since the canzone has a greater range in which it can wander, I do not consider its style as difficult to master as that of the sonnet. And this can be proven easily enough from experience: whoever has composed sonnets and has restricted himself to some given subject matter that is subtle and refined in nature, has only been able to avoid obscurity and harshness of style with great difficulty. There is a big difference between composing sonnets so that the rhymes compel the subject, and composing them so that the subject compels the rhymes. And it seems to me that in Latin verse one has much more latitude than in the vernacular, for in our language, besides metrical feet—which are necessary more because of the nature of verse itself than because of any rule—there is also the problem of the rhyme scheme, which, as all know who have experienced it, interferes with the expression of many wonderful ideas and prevents them from being developed with much clarity or ease. And that our verse has metrical feet of its own is proven by the fact that one could compose any number of verses with eleven syllables without them sounding like verse or being in any other way different from prose.[13] We will conclude from all of this that verse in the vernacular is very difficult, and that among the other verse forms, the composition of the sonnet is the most difficult, and because of this, it is as worthy of being esteemed as any other genre in the vernacular. And yet I do not want to suggest by this argument that my own sonnets have achieved the degree of perfection that I have said is proper to this genre. But, as Ovid says of Phaethon, for the present it suffices that I have attempted that style which excels all other vernacular styles, and if I have not been able to reach perfection in driving this chariot of the sun, at least I might be praised for having dared to attempt this course, even though because of personal deficiencies my strength has not measured up to so great an undertaking.[14]

[*Summary of Omitted Paragraphs*:

In the next paragraphs Lorenzo endeavors to justify the unconventional opening (*principio*) of his exposition, which begins with four sonnets inspired by the death of a woman.[15] This seems unorthodox because death should naturally come at the end of a work, not at its beginning. But since philosophers hold that the corruption of one thing entails the creation of another, it is appropriate that a death should usher in the beginning of his commentary. Moreover, he who lives in love must first die to all other things, for the perfection of love comes from dying to all imperfection. The beginning of true life is the death of the life that is not true. Lorenzo now turns to the exposition of the first four sonnets and their subject.]

Commentary on the First Sonnet

There died, as we have said above, in our city a woman who moved to compassion all the Florentine people. It is no great wonder, for she was truly endowed with as much human beauty and gentilezza as anyone who had ever lived. And among her other excellent gifts, her manner was so sweet and attractive that all those who had any intimate acquaintance with her believed themselves to be deeply loved by her. In fact, neither the women nor young men of her age had any envy of her most excellent and virtuous character. Rather, they praised highly and exalted her beauty and gentilezza, and in such a way that it seemed impossible to believe that so many men could, without jealousy, love her, or that so many women could, without envy, praise her. And though her life, due to her praiseworthy qualities, made her dear to all, yet compassion for her death, because of her tender age and beauty, which even in death may have surpassed that of any living woman, left all with a burning desire for her. And because she was carried from her house to the burial place with her face uncovered, a great abundance of tears flowed from the eyes of all who flocked to see her. Among them, those who had known her felt not only pity but also wonder, for in death she had surpassed that beauty which, while she lived, seemed unsurpassable. Those who had not known her felt a grief approaching remorse, for they had not been able to know her before she was taken from them, but now having seen her, they would ever after grieve for her. In her was truly realized what Petrarch said, "Death itself seemed beautiful in her lovely face."[16]

So, with the death of this woman, and as was fitting for such a public misfortune, all the best minds of Florence grieved in different ways—some in verse, some in prose—over the bitterness of this death, and they strove to praise her as far as their intellectual powers would allow. I, wanting to be in their company as well and to join them in their weeping, composed the following sonnets, the first of which begins "Oh shining star who with your radiance."

It was night, and a very dear friend of mine and I were walking together and talking about this common misfortune. And talking thus, and the heavens being starlit and clear, we directed our gaze toward the west where we clearly saw a very bright star possessing such splendor that it not only outshone by far the other stars but also made, so resplendent it was, those bodies standing in its light cast shadows. Having wondered at this from the outset, I turned to my friend and said, "We should not marvel over this, for the soul of that most noble woman has either been transformed into this new star or else has united with it. If this is true, this brightness no longer seems a wonder. Therefore, just as her beauty, when she was alive, was a great consolation to our eyes, let us now console them with the vision of this very bright star. And if so much light makes our sight weak and frail, let us entreat God—that is, her divine spirit—to strengthen our sight by diminishing to some extent such splendor, so that we may contemplate it for awhile without hurting our eyes. Adorned as it is with the beauty of that woman, this star certainly cannot be accused of presumptuousness for wanting to overcome the splendor of the other stars, since it would even be capable of vying with Phoebus Apollo and asking him for his chariot, in order to become, itself, the creator of day. And if it is true that this star can do this without being presumptuous, it is also true that death has been extremely presumptuous in laying hands on such peerless beauty and virtue." Since this conversation seemed to me very good material for a sonnet, I parted from my friend and composed the present sonnet, in which I speak of the above-mentioned star:

> Oh shining star who with your radiance
> deprives your neighbor stars of all their light,
> why do you blaze so much more than your wont?
> Why do you wish to vie with Phoebus now?
> Perhaps you've gathered up those lovely eyes,
> now taken from us by cruel Death, who does
> presume too much, that with their light you may
> demand of Phoebus his fine chariot.
> Whether we call you this or else a star

newborn who with new radiance adorns
the heavens, grant, oh goddess, these our prayers:
remove enough of your resplendence, so
our eyes, which want to weep eternally,
without another wound may see you happy.

A Commentary on My Sonnets
(the prologue and the first commentary)

Though the earliest parts of "A Commentary" go back to 1473–78, the prologue (*proemio*) was written in 1490–91 (Zanato 11). For the interpretation and significance of the work as a whole, see Lipari and Zanato. Zanato is especially good on Dante's and Ficino's influence, on the sources of the work, and on its important place in Quattrocento criticism. According to Zanato, Lorenzo wrote the sonnet "Oh shining star" in 1476 and its exposition in 1485–86 (325). Our translation is indebted in a number of places to the word choice of Lipari's paraphrase and more generally to Bigi's text and notes (1965). For further remarks on the translation, see my Introduction. For further commentary, see Kennedy 1989, Martelli 1965a, 51–135, and Sturm 25–29, 32–34.

1. There is a gap in the text here. Lorenzo probably wanted to say that though contemplation is the highest occupation, it alone cannot satisfy the necessities of a human life.

2. *one particular person*: this may refer to Pico della Mirandola.

3. In the language of the *dolce stil nuovo, gentilezza* is a technical term meaning much more than gentleness. In Dante it refers to "nobility of soul." Later, in "A Commentary," Lorenzo himself says that something is *gentile* when it can perfectly perform its appropriate function and do so with grace (Bigi 1965, 353). Gentilezza is thus the union of excellence and beauty. See Lipari 111–15.

4. That is, God. See Lorenzo's poem "The Supreme Good," especially capitoli 4 and 5.

5. Lorenzo's persistent use of the terms thing (*cosa*) and object (*subietto*) sounds awkward, but his point is Neoplatonic: the operation of love is global, not just limited to the human plane. See Lipari 13–14n.

6. Petrarch, *Rime* 1.8.

7. "Written with this purpose in mind." I have followed Lipari in interpreting the difficult Italian original of this phrase (20 n. 13).

8. *Guido Cavalcanti*, friend and contemporary of Dante, and a major poet of the *dolce stil nuovo*. Romano and del Garbo were medieval commentators on Cavalcanti's work.

9. A reference to the Pazzi conspiracy (1478), in which Lorenzo's brother was murdered and Lorenzo himself barely escaped with his life. See Acton, passim.

10. *Virtù* has a host of related meanings in Lorenzo's usage, including not only virtue but also strength and excellence.

11. *terza rima* is a verse form composed of triplets whose rhymes interlock (*a b a, b c b*, etc.). It is the verse form of Dante's *Commedia*, hence its epic characteristics, and of a number of Lorenzo's poems (e.g., "The Supreme Good" and "Corinto").

12. I follow here the sense dictated by Simioni's rather than Bigi's punctuation of this sentence.

13. The hendecasyllable, or eleven-syllable line, is the standard line length of much Italian poetry.

14. In Greek myth, Phaethon, son of Helios, asked his father to let him drive the chariot of the sun for a day. He lacked the strength to control the horses, thus endangering the earth, so Zeus struck him dead. Ovid in the second book of his *Metamorphoses* quotes Phaethon's epitaph, which mentions his failure but praises the boldness of his attempt.

15. Simonetta Cataneo, the wife of Marco Vespucci and a famous beauty loved by Giuliano de' Medici and celebrated by many poets, died tragically young in April 1476.

16. Petrarch, "Trionfo della Morte" 1.72.

Corinto

The moon, amid the lesser stars of night,
   shines forth so full through heavens deep and still
   the lustrous stars seem almost lost to sight;   3
and Sleep grants every living soul release
   from all the toils of the daily round,
   and shadows fill the world, and deepest peace.   6
Only Corinto in a wood of beeches
   is singing still for love of Galatea,
   but no one's there to hear this shepherd's speeches.   9
Nor have his eyes enjoyed the least repose
   from weeping; rather, all alone he sings
   in moaning measures of his love and woes.   12
"O Galatea, why have you expressed
   such scorn of sad Corinto, wishing dead
   the shepherd who has always loved you best?   15
Only the woods attend my plaints and sighs,
   and you, Night, hear them too because I dwell
   beneath the mantle of your starry skies.   18
The trusting, well-fed flocks and herds now pass
   their time in quiet bliss, and maybe they
   are chewing still their cuds of pallid grass.   21
The sheep, once more penned up, are at their ease,
   and guarded by the ever-watchful dog,
   they sleep contented in the cooling breeze.   24
Unheard, I now lament my grievous pain
   in dark, despairing words, in cries and pleas,
   but these, unheard, are all expressed in vain.   27
Alas, though she may flee and disappear,
   she does not likewise leave my thoughts, and so
   my heart is wasted more than when she's here.   30

Soften the hardness of your heart, I pray:
  it's fifteen years that you have been a virgin
  under Diana's harsh, unyielding sway!   33
Isn't that time enough? Now come and cheer me,
  nymph, you who've never had a trace of pity.
  But I am cursed. There is no one to hear me.   36
If of a thousand she might hear one word!
  I know that verse can make the moon itself
  come down to earth, provided it is heard.   39
Verse once transformed the sailors of Ulysses
  into beasts, and made the slimy serpent
  upon the greensward split apart in pieces.   42
So let us give the wind this song, severe
  and plain though it may be, for now I know
  the way these plaints of mine shall reach her ear. 45
A breeze will stir the lofty treetops, where
  soft whispers wake, and they will waft her name
  all through the woods and regions of the air.   48
If wind can bring her name to me, it will not fail
  to bring my own complaint to her hard heart
  by way of peaks and through the hollow dale   51
where Echo lives, who seconds all my groans.
  Let Wind or Echo bear my song to her—
  I know it won't be sown among the stones.   54
Perhaps she's listening from some cave nearby.
  Though I'm not sure you're here, I know that I'll
  be close to you, no matter where you fly.   57
If your cruel heart might show some sympathy,
  if only I might find you here and touch
  your hands and lovely face! What ecstasy!   60
If you'd lie down with me upon the lea,
  I'd make some pipes of limber willow bark—
  I'd ask you then to sing, and I would play.   63
Then leafy vines would bind your wanton mane—
  your milky feet would dance and they would kick
  the wind and skip across the grassy plain.   66
Tired, you would lie beneath the oak tree's bower,
  and I would gather flowers in the meadow.
  Over your face I'd drop them in a shower.   69

And there where those I plucked had met their doom
   new flowers of a thousand hues would spring,
   your laugh alone the reason that they bloom.   72
And for your golden tresses I would lace
   many a wreath of leaves and dainty blossoms,
   though you'd surpass them all in natural grace.   75
The songs of amorous birds in lilting measures,
   the murmuring of limpid little brooks,
   would complement the sweetness of our pleasures.   78
The cruelty that's in you, nymph, defy!
   Cast from your heart these bitter thoughts! Do not,
   I beg you, use your charms to make me die!   81
If stalking animals might be your aim,
   you'll find no shepherd more robust or skilled
   than me at giving chase to fleeing game.   84
You, with your bow in hand, without a sound,
   will stay well hid, while I with pointed spear
   await the boar, a little further down.   87
When you, however, flee before my eyes,
   barefoot—alas, what sorrow do I feel
   and how I fear, while sighing many sighs,   90
that thorn or precipice or poison snake
   will hurt your feet, which I would hate. In vain,
   I raise my feet with yours or make them brake,   93
like one who aims and lets an arrow go,
   then cranes his neck to guide it to the mark
   although the shaft's already left the bow.   96
But you're so light and quick that I would bet
   your buoyancy would let you run across
   the water, and your feet would not get wet.   99
But then my heart receives an awful fright:
   that you might imitate Narcissus—he
   whose charms afforded him too much delight—   102
when, having bathed your face down by the spring,
   you stare into the water's tranquil mirror
   after the swirls have finished settling.   105
How slow, how foolish is the lover's mind!
   You leave. I race up to the pool, forgetting
   your lovely likeness hasn't stayed behind.   108

I peer into the pool but do not see
    you there. I see myself, and so become
    convinced that you might not disdain my plea.   111
If I am swarthy, blame the sun: I am
    a robust shepherd, so it fits. Now tell me,
    what good's a man who doesn't have a tan?   114
If on my back and chest the hair is dense,
    this fact will not displease you, if you have
    as much good sense and taste as elegance.   117
Nor do you know the measure of my might:
    when I lay hold of some wild bullock's horns,
    I throw him to the ground, in his despite.   120
I went inside a gloomy cave the other day
    so as to snatch a pair of baby bears.
    I had to use my hands to find the way.   123
Reaching the place, I dragged them from their lair.
    The mother bear then heard me—proud and mad
    she came toward me with threatening air.   126
Seizing a sturdy branch with which to strike,
    I left her lifeless in the grass, then took
    the cubs, which I will give you if you like.   129
I vanquish all who wrestle man to man,
    and that is how I won two days ago
    a cow and heifer at the feast of Pan.   132
With bow in hand, I went to test my worth
    against Diana—and won a four-horned ram
    whose snowy mantle reaches to the earth.   135
Let it be yours, though this offend Neifil,
    who preens herself for me in vain—to whom,
    alas, for love of you, I've been so cruel.   138
Whether or not I'm rich, you'll learn by heeding
    how every side of every vale resounds
    with cattle lowing, and with sheep flocks bleating.   141
Fresh milk I have, and on the flowery mead
    strawberries fair and plump and red, which seem,
    against your cheek's high color, wan indeed;   144
and fruits of every season, large, mature;
    thousands of bees, so many thousands that
    you'd hardly think the world had room for more.   147

Their honey is so sweet that it must be
   like the ambrosia Jove may eat—and sweeter
   than any sugar cane from Sicily.   150
If you're not moved, oh nymph, by my lament,
   at least be moved then by the songs of birds,
   whose voices sing of sorrow, yet enchant.   153
Can you not hear the way poor Filomen,
   like me, does grieve from love—how she, as I
   of you, in sweetest verses does complain?   156
Her song alone now keeps me company.
   Pity I try to rouse in you. I bathe
   the ground with tears. And you just laugh at me. 159
Where sovereign beauty joins with cruel disdain
   there lodges living death—but I take comfort:
   some day your beauty will begin to wane.   162
I went one morning to my garden site—
   by then the rising sun was radiant,
   although not all of it was yet in sight—   165
and planted there were rose trees, two or more.
   I turned, wide-eyed, to look at them—I stared
   because I'd never noticed them before.   168
Red roses, also white, I saw that day.
   Sunstruck, one rose unfurls its fettered petals,
   then blossoms forth in blowzy disarray.   171
Another, younger, stands almost revealed
   outside its bud. And here is one that still
   shuts out the air, its petals tightly sealed.   174
Another, falling down, adorns the ground.
   And so I saw it all, their birth, their death,
   their beauty ruined in an hour's round.   177
And when I saw those pallid petals wither
   and fall upon the earth, it dawned on me
   how brief it is that youth remains in flower. 180
Each tree receives its blooms; and tender leaves
   soon after open to the sun, for now
   they feel the presence of the warming breeze. 183
The tiny fruits, still shapeless, then expand
   and gradually some grow so big that from
   their weight the stoutest branches sag and bend. 186

These limbs cannot, without grave risk, sustain
   their own great weight, but since they grow so slow
   they nearly get accustomed to the strain.   189
Autumn returns. The sweet ripe fruit is picked.
   The days of warmth and sunshine pass away.
   The trees, of flowers, fruit, and leaves, are stripped.   192
Gather the rose, oh nymph, now while you may."

Corinto

With "Corinto" we have the first of Lorenzo's three great mythological poems. As with the "Ambra" and the second "Wood of Love," this mythological eclogue reveals a much more intensive use of the classical tradition than the earlier poems.

Along with influences from Dante, Petrarch, Boccaccio, and love poetry of a more popular nature, there are strong echoes from Theocritus's *Idylls*, Virgil's *Eclogues*, Ovid's *Metamorphoses*, Horace, and Ausonius (see Maier 1949). Yet for all of its complex intertextuality, this lovely poem gives the effect of freshness and original inspiration. This is because Lorenzo has been able to "naturalize" his classical sources, giving them a Tuscan setting and atmosphere (Sturm 95). By uniting classical sources with popular, indigenous traditions, he was able in the "Corinto" and his other classical poems to endow myths with a concreteness and immediacy rarely found in earlier treatments (Maier 1969, 36).

"Corinto" was composed in the mid-1480s (no later than 1486), a period in which Lorenzo was especially close to Poliziano, who probably helped inspire the classical turn in Lorenzo's poetry. I have used the standard text reprinted in Bigi 1965.

28.   *though she may flee*: that is, the nymph Galatea.
33.   *under Diana's harsh sway*: that is, under the rule of Diana, virgin goddess of the hunt, scorner of men.
40–41.   *Verse once transformed the sailors of Ulysses*, etc.: a reference to the episode in the *Odyssey* where the men of Odysseus (Ulysses) are transformed into swine by the goddess-enchantress Circe.

52.   *Echo*: a nymph who loved Narcissus (see below) and whose speech could only echo that of others.

101.   *Narcissus*: a self-centered youth who fell in love with his own reflection in the water and either died of unrequited love for it or drowned in pursuit of it.

154.   *Filomen*: she was changed into a nightingale after Tereus seduced her and cut out her tongue. The nightingale's song is her sad plaint.

163–93. This section is a vivid vernacularization of Ausonius's "De rosis nascentibus."

Ambra

Part I

1. Fled is the time of year that turned the flowers
    Into ripe apples, long since gathered in.
    The leaves, no longer cleaving to the boughs,
    Lie strewn throughout the woods, now much less dense,
    And rustle should a hunter pass that way,
    A few of whom will sound like many more.
    Though the wild beast conceals her wandering tracks,
    She cannot cross those brittle leaves unheard.

2. Among the leafless trees, the verdant laurel
    Stands alongside the fragrant Cyprian myrtle,
    And firs rise green against the alpine whiteness,
    And bend their branches loaded down with snow.
    The cypress hides within itself some birds.
    The robust pine does battle with the winds,
    And lowly junipers keep prickly leaves
    Yet spare the hand that plucks them carefully.

3. On some mild, sunny slope the olive seems
    Now white, now green, according to the wind:
    So nature in the olive tree sustains
    The greenery that fails in other leaves.
    Already with much toil the migrant birds
    Have led their weary families beyond
    The sea, and on the way had shown them Tritons
    And Nereids and other prodigies.

4. The Night, who battled for supremacy
    And won, consigns to jail the short-lived Day:

Through cloudless heavens bound by ceaseless flames
She blithely leads the starry wain around.
And Night won't come until that other golden
Beautiful wain descends beneath the sea.
Menaced by cold Orion's knife, bright Phoebus
Dares not display to us his splendid face.

5. Not far behind the blazing wain of Night
Go wakefulness and sharp anxiety,
Then potent sleep—who yet must many times
Be overthrown by these tenacious cares—
And soothing dreams that stealthily beguile
The mind oppressed by great adversities:
Dreaming of health and wealth consoles the one
Who's sick and destitute when he awakes.

6. Wretched is he who, stung by sweet desire
That longed-for day has promised to fulfill,
Lies sleepless through the long-enduring night
And ardently awaits for day to come!
And though in wakefulness or even sleep
He may exclude sad thoughts and welcome glad,
And though he shuts his eyes to cheat the time,
Yet night will seem to him a hundred years.

7. Wretched is he who finds himself at sea,
Far from the shore on such an endless night
When wind disrupts his blinded vessel's course
And the sea shakes and raves with savage roars.
Although invoked by many prayers and vows,
Aurora tarries with her ancient mate.
The sailor watches avidly, and sadly
Reckons, the sluggish steps of tardy Night.

8. How different, how opposite, the fate
Of happy lovers during winter's frost,
For whom the nights seem all too bright and brief,
While day drags on too gloomy and too long.
The song birds, clad anew in winter's plumes

Against the time of ice and bitter cold,
Have laid aside their songs, whose drift, if gay
Or dolorous, I never seem to catch.

9. And from afar the honking cranes imprint
The skies with lovely, variegated shapes—
The one behind extends its neck to reach
The empty tracks the crane ahead has made.
And once the flock attains the sunny plains,
One bird stands guard, the others rest asleep.
A thousand kinds of many-colored fowl
Cover the fields and float across the lakes.

10. And often will the eagle slowly glide
Above the water, menacing the throng:
The cranes rise up as one and drive it hence
Before a blast of loudly beating wings,
But should one crane forsake the feathered flock,
The agile eagle quickly swoops it up:
The victim is deceived if it believes
That it is borne to Jove like Ganymede.

11. Zephyr has fled to cheerful Cyprian meadows
And dances, leisurely, with Flora there.
Here, Aquilon and Boreas disturb
And agitate the tranquil, golden air.
The babbling stream, made crystalline by ice,
Now lies in rest, all weary and serene.
A hard, pellucid wave immures the fish
The same way golden amber holds a fly.

12. That peak which stops fierce Coro's wind from harming
The noble flower, grown to honor, wealth
And ruling power in Morello's lap,
Now wreathes his head, already white, with mist.
Cascading down that haughty head, the hoary
Locks cover up his shoulders. Stiff with ice,
The shaggy beard conceals his hairy chest.
The eyes and nose become a fount, then freeze.

13. Moist Noto sets upon his head the cloudy
     Garland that circles round his lofty temples.
     Then alpine Boreas drives the crown away
     To leave the ancient head all white and bare.
     Noto, on damp malignant wings, brings back
     The fog, and clothes the mountain once again.
     Laden or light, Morello thus in wrath
     Threatens the plain by turns with snow and rain.

14. The hot and murky Auster takes his leave
     Of Ethiopia, and in the salty
     Tyrrhenian waves he slakes his thirsty sponges.
     Worn out and wrapped in water-bloated clouds,
     He barely makes his destined resting place
     Before he squeezes both his spongy fists.
     To meet the friendly rains, rejoicing streams
     Now issue freely from their ancient caves.

15. Their temples graced with fluvial leaves and weeds,
     The rivers render Father Ocean thanks,
     And sound in joy their hoarse and twisted horns.
     The proud and swollen belly swells the more—
     Their wrath, which has been building up for days
     Against the frightened banks, now finds a vent.
     The frothing stream has breached the hostile dike
     And spurns the bounds of ancient riverbeds.

16. Not by protracted routes or winding paths
     That look like serpents' ample coils do they,
     The rivers, make their way to their old sire.
     Far, distant rivers let their waves converge,
     And each one tells the other, like a friend,
     The news and customs of his native land,
     And so together, with outlandish voices,
     They search, in vain, for their lost estuaries.

17. When a wide-reaching, swollen stream is forced
     Inside a gorge enclosed by mountain flanks,
     Its vicious waters, troubled, braking, hiss,

And mixed with mud give off a yellow hue.
Raging against the narrow alley's rocks,
The torrent tumbles boulder over boulder,
And swirls the foaming waves and wildly quakes:
The herdsman, peering down secure, yet fears.

18. Such mournful quakings wrack the wretched earth
Deep down inside her scorched and hollow bowels,
And through her narrow mouth she tosses forth
A fount of flame and steamy smoke whose roar
Appalls the ear, whose sight affrights the eye.
Nearby, Volterra, high and fast, still fears
That sound, and fears her foaming, troubled springs,
And when their smoke is higher, looks for rain.

19. Likewise distressed, the full, ferocious torrent
Rages, and, swollen, mauls the hostile banks,
But once stretched out upon the spacious plain
He barely can be heard and seems content,
Unsure if he descends or flows upstream,
He who had made a shore of distant peaks.
Laden with alpine loot, with limbs and trunks,
The victor now draws near the peaceful lake.

20. The frightened peasant woman barely has
The time to free the creatures from their stall;
She takes her wailing baby in his crib;
Her older daughter follows, shoulders laden
With heaps of homespun wool and linen cloth;
The other household goods all float about;
The pigs and panic-stricken oxen swim;
Later, the flock of sheep will not be shorn.

21. One member of the family has retreated
Onto the rooftop of the house, from where
He sees go under all their meager wealth,
Their toil, their hope. So much he fears for his
Own life, he cannot grieve or speak aloud.
Within his heavy breast his heart fears death,

And takes no count of things, however dear:
The greater care thus drives all others out.

22.   The green, familiar banks no longer curb
      The happy fish, who have more ample room,
      Their just and ancient wish to see new shores,
      Somewhat appeased, but not fulfilled. And this
      New pleasure leads them gladly forth to see
      Great ruins and the wrecks of monuments.
      They thrill to see the walls beneath the waves,
      Ramparts that even now they dare not trust.

Part II

23.   During this time of year, Ombrone, a lover
      Swollen and proud encircles Ambra, she
      Like a small island. Ambra, no less dear
      To Lauro, jealous if his rival hugs her.
      Ambra, the wood nymph, Delia's favorite
      Of those who send the arrow from the bow.
      So fair and fine she finally wounds the god.
      And light of foot, the swiftest of the nymphs.

24.   Kind, gentle Lauro, shepherd of the alps,
      Had loved with purest love this dryad since
      Her tender years, nor had the flame of lust
      Invaded Lauro's rare and noble breast.
      One day, to flee the heat, she bathed unclothed
      In cold Ombrone's waters, he whose looks
      And manners proud stem from his ancient sire,
      Apennine, and a hundred brother streams.

25.   When she immersed her maiden members in
      His dark, cold stream, Ombrone felt them, and,
      Excited by her body's grace and lightness,
      The haughty godling issued from his cave.
      His left hand taking up his twisted horn,

He stands quite naked, ardent with desire,
And crowned with fronds of fir and mountain beech,
He shields his tousled head from Phoebus's rays.

26. Hid by the fronds, he softly, slowly steals
Up to the pool in which the wood nymph stands.
She fails to see him, and the murmurings
Of lambent waves drown out the sound of steps.
So near, so close to her has he advanced,
He feels he now can reach her golden tresses,
And have that comely nymph within his arms,
And, naked, clasp her naked lovely body.

27. Just as a fish—above which some unseen
Fisherman spreads his subtle, fine-spun web—
First feels, then flees the net that floats above
And in its flight abandons several scales,
So too the nymph on seeing that she's seen,
Escapes the god, who flings himself against her:
Yet she was slow enough, or he so swift,
She left with him a handful of her hair.

28. So springing from the waves, she speeds her pace—
Barefoot and naked, full of fear she flees,
Leaving behind her arrows, clothes, and quiver,
Careless of prickly thorns or jagged rocks.
The wretched godling, weary, stays his step.
He wrings his hands, he gazes at the sky,
And when he sees those torn-out, flaxen hairs,
He execrates his cruel and sluggish hand.

29. And then, pursuing her, he says: Oh hand
So fierce, so quick to tear away her lovely
Tresses, you were, alas, not quick enough
To seize her godlike form, to give me bliss.
Thus having rued in vain his first mistake,
And thinking speech at least might reach that place
His sluggish steps cannot attain, he shouts:
Oh nymph, I am a river, yet I burn!

30. Among these chilly waves, you have inflamed
    My heart and breast with burning, blind desire.
    So why not lie with me, just as you lay
    Within my waves? It would be even better,
    For if you liked my limpid waves and shade,
    More lovely still are those inside my cave.
    My things delight you, I delight you not,
    Yet I'm the son of Apennine—a god!

31. The wood nymph flees. She's deaf to all his pleas,
    And fear puts wings upon her ivory feet.
    The god runs on and quickens now his pace,
    Made swifter in pursuit by power of love.
    To his great grief he sees those ivory feet
    Wounded by thorns and by the sharp-edged stones.
    Seeing the lovely, naked nymph escape,
    His passion swells, he freezes, and he sweats.

32. Afraid, ashamed, the nymph still runs away—
    Her running overcomes the rapid winds.
    Her nimble soles might step on top of ears
    Of wheat, and these would bear her gentle feet.
    Ombrone sees he always loses ground.
    He sees the nymph grow small with every step:
    Once on the plain, she moves so far ahead,
    He loses hope of catching up with her.

33. Before, he'd come through steep and rugged mountains
    Where he had swiftly run between the rocks.
    Less agile steps, there, slowed her pace, and raised
    His hopes for some advantage and relief,
    But when, alas, he reached the open plains,
    These almost reined the tired river in.
    And since his feet cannot keep up with her,
    With lustful eyes he now pursues the nymph.

34. What should the smitten godling do, now that
    He can no longer catch the comely nymph?
    The more she is denied to him, the more

Desire inflames and stings his smitten heart.
The nymph's already close to where my Arno
Receives Ombron, whose waves he joins with his;
Seeing the Arno cheers Ombrone so,
His ruined hopes begin again to rise.

35.   From far he shouts: Oh Arno, into whom
      Most of us Tuscan rivers pour our waters,
      That lovely nymph who birdlike flies from me,
      Whom I pursued through many woods and mountains,
      Mercilessly this nymph torments my heart,
      Nor does her own hard heart, it seems, know love:
      Restore lost hope, deliver her to me,
      Obstruct and interrupt her rapid flight!

36.   Ombron am I, and I collect my azure
      Waters for you: for you they're all reserved.
      They so increase your waters' depths, that high
      And swollen you disdain both banks and bridges.
      This nymph's my prize, my prey; these golden tresses
      That in my hand with bitter grief I hold
      Tell all; my only hope resides in you:
      Assist me quickly since the wood nymph flies.

37.   Not having time enough to give an answer,
      Hearing Ombron and moved by pity, Arno
      Holds back his waves. Already large and swollen,
      He hinders from afar fair Ambra's course.
      Once more cold terror strikes the virgin's breast,
      The closer she approaches Arno's shore:
      Behind she hears Ombron, in front's a lake,
      Nor does her doubtful heart know where to turn.

38.   Just as a hunted beast pursued by hounds,
      Who, losing them, eludes their avid mouths,
      And now released from danger, sees, aghast,
      The gaping net ahead before its eyes,
      And nearly sure it must get caught, will not
      Advance in flight, dares not retrace its path,

But dreads the hounds, mistrusts the net, and knows
Not where to turn, and, full of fear, cries out:

39. So too the lovely nymph, and such her fate.
     From here, from there, borne hard upon by horror,
     All she can do is yearn for death. She sees
     Both rivers closing in on her, and losing
     All hope, resoundingly, the nymph cries out:
     Oh goddess chaste, to whom my cherished father
     And aged mother consecrated me,
     Unique one, help me in this final trial!

40. Diana fair, not yet has mad desire
     Defiled this virgin breast: protect it now,
     Since I, a nymph, alone cannot repulse
     Two enemies, each one of them a god.
     All that my heart retains, besides the longing
     For death, is pure, unblemished love of Lauro.
     Convey to him, oh winds, these final words,
     So that my Lauro may bemoan my fate.

41. These words had hardly issued from her mouth
     When both of her white feet were seized by an
     Unusual rigidity. You see
     Them grow and turn to stone. You see the color
     Of legs and lovely torso change, and yet
     You would believe this was a woman still:
     Her limbs look like a human figure sketched,
     But left unfinished, in the solid stone.

42. Though weary from the race he'd run thus far,
     Ombron revives, accelerates his pace
     In hopes of capturing the precious prey,
     And seems to think she's nearly in his arms.
     Seeing the rock increase before his eyes,
     He has no inkling yet from where it comes.
     But then he sees how vain his hope has been:
     He pulls up short, amazed and full of grief.

43. When brought to bay by hounds inside a park
    Enclosed by fences or a modest wall,
    Some hind or beast will lose all hope of flight,
    And near the wall, spurred on by fear, will jump,
    Ascending gracefully before the dogs,
    Who sad and disappointed stay behind.
    Unable to pursue her soaring course,
    They stop, they stare at where she got away.

44. Just so, Ombrone stops his hasty steps,
    And, wretched, sees the shapely, growing rock,
    Which still suggests a lovely woman's form,
    Which seems to feel a little something yet.
    As love and pity animate his heart
    He bathes the stone with bitter tears, and says:
    These waters, oh my nymph, are those in which
    You once were pleased to bathe your charming body.

45. I never would have thought, in such distress,
    That my self-pity—overcome by that
    My nymph deserved—might fade to some extent:
    The greater pity for my lovely Ambra,
    Not sorrow for myself, now makes me weep.
    And yet, on second thought, my sad and sordid
    Life, though immortal, is a fate far worse
    Than hers, for she no longer feels a thing.

46. Alas! Up in my father's lofty mountains
    Are many nymphs, each one carefree—somehow
    I chose the one most beautiful among
    A thousand beauties. Loving her alone,
    I tore some hair from her, first pledge of love,
    And drove her from my cool, dark waters.
    Then fleeing, pale and soft and naked, she
    Stained with her sacred blood the stones and thorns.

47. At last she was transmuted into rock,
    For which the only cause was my cruel lust.
    How did I lose her, whom I never had,

I who can never lose the life I have?
My fate in this is too severe, to be
A god—immortal, and in misery!
Whereas, if I could die at least, this great
And everlasting grief would also cease.

48. I've learned just how to please the one I loved,
     And how to win her love, this woman who,
     The more she's loved, the more she is displeased.
     Oh icy Boreas, freeze my current, turn
     My coursing waters into solid ice,
     That, petrified, I can attend the nymph.
     And may the sun with shining golden shafts
     Nevermore melt my hardened, crystal waves.

Ambra

Probably written after 1486 (Bigi 1965, 477), "Ambra" is perhaps the finest Ovidian poem of the Quattrocento. The work is indebted to the Arethusa episode in Ovid's *Metamorphoses* and to Ovidian poems by Boccaccio and Luca Pulci. Lorenzo owned at Poggio a Caiano a villa named "Ambra." The poem is thus an etiological myth explaining the origin of the site of the villa and its name (cf. the earlier Latin work by Poliziano, also entitled "Ambra"). In the Laurentian myth, the wood nymph Ambra is chased by Ombrone, who is both a god and a river (the one flowing behind Lorenzo's estate). Before Ombrone can seize her, Ambra is transformed into a rocky eminence (near the river), the future site of Lorenzo's villa. Hence, the shepherd Lauro's (Lorenzo's) jealousy whenever the river "hugs" Ambra, that is, whenever Ombrone's floodwaters embrace the villa (stanza 23).

   The first part of the poem (stanzas 1–22) is a richly detailed description of the Tuscan landscape in winter and, then, in the spring flood season. The raging rivers of the first part prepare the reader for the tempestuous passion of Ombrone for Ambra in the second part (stanzas 23–48). For the controversy over the *non finito* status of the poem and the relation of its two parts, see Bessi 1986, "Un opera aperta?", Sturm 108–9, and my Introduction, part IV.

For the translation, I have consulted both Bigi 1965 and Bessi's critical edition (1986), as well as Chastel's French and Stange's German versions of the poem.

1.1.   *Fled is the time of year*: autumn has ended and winter has begun.

2.1.   *the verdant laurel*: a pun on one form of Lorenzo's name, Lauro (which is also the name of Ambra's faithful lover in the second section of the poem; see 24). The laurel associations also link the poem to Ovid's metamorphosis myth of Apollo's attempted rape of Daphne, who is turned into a laurel tree at the last minute. On the political implications of the laurel and its verdancy, see the Introduction, part I.

4.3.   *ceaseless flames*: a reference to the empyrean of medieval and Renaissance cosmology, i.e., the sphere of pure fire encompassing the heavens.

4.4.   *the starry wain*: the constellation of *Ursa major*, also known as the Wagon or Wain.

4.6–7. *that other golden beautiful wain*: that is, the chariot of the sun.

4.7.   *menaced by cold Orion's knife, bright Phoebus*: threatened by the knife of the constellation Orion, Phoebus, the sun, does not rise.

7.6.   *Aurora tarries with her ancient mate*: Aurora, the dawn, stays in bed with her lover, Tithonus, rather than rising.

10.8.   *That it is borne to Jove like Ganymede*: Jove, enamored of the boy Ganymede, took the form of an eagle and swooped the lad up to Olympus, where he served as the cupbearer of the gods.

11.1–4. Zephyr, the gentle warm west wind, has gone to Cyprus, where he dances with Flora, goddess of flowers (cf. Botticelli's *Primavera*). Meanwhile, back in Tuscany, the chill north winds Aquilon and Boreas have come.

11.8.   *a fly*: mosquito, in the original.

12.1–2. *That peak . . . The noble flower*: The peak, Mount Morello, near Florence (*the noble flower*), blocks the Coro, a northwest wind.

13.1.   *Moist Noto*: a humid wind from the south.

14.1.   *The hot and murky Auster*: a south wind, dark with dust or moisture.

14.3.   *Tyrrhenian waves*: the Tyrrhenian Sea lies southwest of Italy.

15.3.   *twisted horns*: symbol of the river gods, who come out of their ancient caves and thank Father Ocean, because he is the source of their waters.

16.3.   *their old sire*: the ocean.

18.1–8.   A comparison of the violence of the spring torrent to volcanic action and to the volatile mineral springs of the Tuscan hill town of Volterra.

19.6.   The river had filled up whole valleys with detritus, thus making peaks into shores.

23.1–2.   *Ombrone . . . Ambra*: Ombrone, the river god, floods and encircles the rocky eminence, Ambra, site of Lorenzo's (Lauro's) villa.

23.5.   *Delia*: Diana, virgin goddess of the hunt.

24.8.   *Apennine*: refers both to the mountain range and its tutelary god.

34.5.   *my Arno*: a major Tuscan river, of which Ombrone is a tributary.

41.1–8.   On the relation of this stanza and its sculptural simile to Lorenzo's aesthetic, see the Introduction, part IV.

A Wood of Love II (selections)

Spring

20. And you will see, as if it were in spring,
    The slopes decked out in many different hues.
    The earth, no longer plagued by bitter weather,
    Will clothe herself with violets and roses,
    And the new sun will make those constellations
    Opposed to warmer days benign and gentle.
    The frosty season, raw and lingering,
    Will not, on looking, recognize himself.

21. Winter, surprised and gratified, will see
    The dry bare limbs reclothed with little leaves,
    The pointed twigs changed into pretty flowers,
    The swallow and the nightingale returned.
    He'll see the bees deserting their old hives
    And buzzing merrily from bloom to bloom;
    And, taking tiny steps, sagacious ants
    Resuming now their interrupted tasks.

22. The kindly shepherd in this gentle season
    Leads from their winter stalls his bleating flock
    Which presses in a joyous throng as it
    Returns to mountain meads and clear cool streams.
    The lambkin, tripping lightly, follows in
    Its mother's tracks; the loving shepherd bears
    Another in his arms, just newly born.
    The faithful dog escorts them, one and all.

23. Another shepherd carries on his shoulders
    A sheep that's lame, and yet another, on

A pregnant mare, has slung across its rump
The netting, mallet, and the other tools
With which to pen the sheep when it grows dark:
In that way none will stumble on a wolf.
The happy shepherds sup on junket pies
And cottage cheese, then snore the whole night through.

24.   The birds will break the silences of night,
       Less long of late, by singing in the boughs:
       One bird, it seems, is adding bits of straw
       And twigs to what is left of last year's nest.
       The mushrooms of the greensward will stand out,
       And merry women now will gather them.
       The dormouse, waking up, will leave its hole,
       And in the evening you will hear the owl.

25.   And you'll see Flora—who of late's been gone—
       Back in her kingdoms, roaming with her nymphs:
       Her lover Zephyr holds her in his arms
       And they go frolicking with one another.
       By virtue of unusual powers, Winter
       Will crown his hoary mane with greenery;
       Wild tigers, bears, and lions will grow tame;
       And waters bound in ice will flow again.

26.   Clytie will leave her ancient lover, slowly
       Turning her pallid face another way.
       Toward this new ardent rising in the east
       The throngs of other flowers point their faces,
       Intent on gazing at and worshiping
       The splendid light that issues from her eyes.
       The dewdrops on the grass, on every sprig,
       No longer nourish Phoebus's bright rays.

27.   And you will hear resound throughout the green,
       Well-shaded valleys, horns and bagpipes, made
       From willow bark or chestnut—you will see
       Dances at noon beneath the shade of elms.
       The fish below the limpid waves will feel

The power of those lovely eyes; and with
His daughters, Nereus will have calm seas.
The joyous world will wear another face.

28. Just as a sapling with a well-done graft
Will marvel when it sees grow out of it
Exotic blooms and leaves and strange new fruits
That ripen and are fed upon its stock,
So too will icy Winter be astounded
When lovely Earth reveals herself to us
Attired in a new, enchanting gown:
He'll ask, "Have I become a child again?"

32. And satyrs, sprightly skipping, crowned with leaves
Will come to venerate my lovely sun;
And piping Pan will come, attended by
His fauns, who bear green boughs from alpine trees;
And nymphs who carry in their laps and baskets
Pale violets and roses glistening white;
And river gods, adorned with tender weeds,
Who fill their twisted horns with blooms and sprigs.

Jealousy

39. Only an aged woman—pallid, speechless,
And sighing—took her seat in a dark nook
In order to avoid the sun. She wears
A mantle of uncertain, changing color.
This wicked goddess has a hundred ears
And eyes, and every eye produces tears.
She never sleeps, she trusts herself alone,
And everything she sees and hears is sad.

40. When at the dawn of time, old Chaos bore
His charming son Amor, this evil goddess
Of whom I speak was born as well: Amor
And Jealousy thus shared a common birth.

But Jove, the kindly father, gracious to
The world, expelled her to the shadow realm
With Pluto and the Furies: there she dwelled
While Saturn and the Age of Gold prevailed.

41.   Then the immortal gods, incensed because
       They'd been so often and so deeply hurt
       By cruel Amor—now falling in some snare,
       Or in some other trap of his—made *her*
       Come back from Hades, by divine decree,
       And stay with Love, wherever he might be.
       That's why this foe infests the world. To Love
       She'll always be as shadow is to body.

42.   The sovereign father, Jove, had deeply feared
       That given his new powers, Chaos's sweet
       Seductive son might well supplant him as
       The head of parliament, consigning him,
       His rule and scepter, to some other realm.
       So Jove himself revoked her banishment
       And at the Stygian swamp he pledged an oath
       That she must ever follow in Love's tracks.

43.   By means of her the sovereign father thought
       To take away the force of Cupid's darts,
       And loosen the hard knots and snares of love.
       For he had seen what pain and suffering
       The never-dying gods who fell in love
       Endured: what sighs, what tears, what pangs and torments
       Each thought of love provoked. And he had seen
       Them flee Love's harsh regime and heavy yoke.

44.   No sooner, though, had oath and ordinance
       Been sanctioned by the parliament of gods
       Than Jove was discontent with what he'd done,
       Repenting, though too late, the oath he'd sworn:
       He, too, by now had felt this mortal woe.
       Before this, love had brought delight, without

Distrust. If he had not already promised,
He would have sent her back to Tartarus.

45. First born of Chaos, nourished then by Pluto,
Oh wicked spirit, with the milk of Furies,
She makes all living mortals feel the woes
Of that great realm where light does not exist.
She deals a mortal wound that never heals
With a sword stained in froth from Cerberus,
Who dwells down in the netherworld. She always
Conceives the worst, and takes what's good as ill.

46. She feeds on evil thoughts and foolish phantoms.
Her grievous maw forever gnaws the heart,
And once consumed, the heart is then renewed.
Wretched is he who's born to such a fate:
Already in the crib his doleful breast
Will overflow with jealousy and hate.
But when my lovely Sun draws near, she flees,
Though never disappears, this living death.

Hope

67. A lady of enormous height she is,
Whose crown of hair appears to touch the sky.
Composed of densest fog and clothed in it,
She dwells among the highest peaks. A man
Who stares at clouds conceives, and thinks he sees,
The wondrous shapes of moving creatures, which
The wind dissolves and forms anew. So Love,
When he depicts this insubstantial dame.

68. Lovely she seems and at a distance tall.
Her shadow covers nearly all the world.
If someone who's in love approaches her,
She gradually grows thin and vanishes
Just as a cloud will disappear from sight

When stinging Boreas is wont to blow.
So though she's never where you think she'll be,
She always can be seen before your eyes.

69.　As when a dog, who hopes to bathe his avid
　　　Maw in the blood of some escaping beast,
　　　Cannot quite reach the creature, just beyond
　　　His grasp, but yearns to catch it all the same,
　　　Just so our foolish longing won't be stilled
　　　But stays as hungry as it ever was.
　　　The beast is swifter, always keeps the lead,
　　　While he, who's eaten up by longing, raves.

70.　This lover's like someone who, with the sun
　　　Behind his back, would overtake his shadow
　　　Or else catch up with it: the shadow must
　　　Precede him, though, regardless of his speed.
　　　So let him run as swiftly as a stag,
　　　He'll still remain as far behind as ever:
　　　It seems he gains on it and moves ahead,
　　　But when the race is run, he's still the last.

71.　An ox or horse that pulls a cart along
　　　Can never reach the ever-turning wheels:
　　　It's no more likely that you'll catch this woman.
　　　Her empty face no mortal eye can see.
　　　Her only eye looks forward, never backward,
　　　And gazes on remote, exalted things.
　　　Only Minerva with her shield has seen
　　　That face: she finds our anguish laughable.

72.　Two feathered wings, immense beyond all measure,
　　　Ascend above her cloud-enshrouded shoulders.
　　　She soars up to the heights from where all those
　　　Who thought she sent them there come tumbling down.
　　　This beast devours wind and empty phantoms
　　　And hardly ever sups on other fare.
　　　She only flies at night, and like the Dawn,
　　　She always flees the splendor of the sun.

73. Heaven and Pluto drove this woman hence:
    She flies now through the regions in between,
    Where Juno turns the vapors into hail,
    And makes the heavy clouds dissolve in rain;
    Where Vulcan fashions bolts to fill his quiver
    And Aquilon and Zephyr loose their winds;
    Where comets, lightning, falling stars are seen,
    And lovely Iris with her thousand colors.

74. Omens and Dreams and Falsehoods file behind
    This luckless dame wherever she may go,
    Along with palmists, frauds of every kind,
    Diviners, lots, and lying prophecies—
    Declaimed or written out on silly cards
    Foretelling, when it's past, what yet will be—
    Astrology and alchemy as well,
    And wild conjectures always made at will.

75. The murky shadows of her ample wings
    Give refuge to the vain and foolish world.
    Oh wretched blindness of humanity!
    Oh ignorance so proud and yet pathetic!
    He who could count the woes she brings could count
    The stars above, the fishes in the ocean,
    The birds who cross the seas in fall, and all
    The leaves that flutter down from naked trees.

The Golden Age

84. Before Prometheus hatched the baneful scheme
    Of perpetrating his outrageous theft,
    The peaceful world was justly ruled by Saturn
    During the epoch of the Golden Age.
    Our human life was longer, happier,
    And truth and its appearance were the same.
    Desire, then, was moderate, content,
    And no one knew the words for "yours" and "mine."

85. And what the bounteous earth gave forth was shared
    By all in common in that happy age.
    Unscathed by plow or hoe, the land produced
    A multitude of fruits and grains and clothed
    Itself in flowers and in fragrant grasses
    Which sun or ice would never devastate.
    The joyous, rushing waters, sweet and clear,
    Allayed a thirst not yet intemperate.

86. Upon the grassy leas the happy herds
    Were unconfined and wandered fearlessly:
    The timid shepherd did not dread that they'd
    Be seized and carried off by wolves or bears.
    In those days many bulls were still untamed
    And hadn't yet been robbed of passion's heat.
    Nor did their necks display hard callouses
    That come from endless hours beneath the yoke.

87. And on some stubbly pasture one would see
    A ewe, contented, grazing near a wolf,
    And neither one would show a trace of fear.
    No wolves were fierce, no sheep were ever scared.
    Nor was the fox malevolent and sly:
    The peasant woman had no need to keep
    A snarling dog to drive it from her hens,
    And when it came she greeted it with joy.

88. The hound and rabbit shared a single bush:
    One did not bark, the other did not squeal.
    Peace reigned between the greyhound, stag, and deer,
    And speed was not a source of hope or fear.
    Sometimes they'd romp about and, then, they liked
    To tease each other: if they ran, it wasn't
    In order to escape some mortal bite,
    But only to gain victory in the race.

89. Snow white and innocent, without a taint,
    The happy dove could nest just where she liked,
    Quite unafraid that other envious doves

Of either sex might devastate her eggs.
She didn't fear the falcon in the fields
Or goshawks' ambuscades among the trees.
The flying heron screeching with delight
Did not yet fear the taloned falcon's strike.

90. The partridge did not dread that tercel's claws
Would seize her like sharp pincers grabbing iron.
The heavy quail, when rising up in flight,
Feared not that she'd be captured by a hawk.
The merlin felt delight when singing larks
Soared up into the heavens from the ground.
And serpents were not fearful in the least
That they'd end up as food for baby storks.

91. And you could amble barefoot through the grass
But not get bitten by a cold-skinned snake.
The vipers, lacking venom, did not hiss
Or cause the heart to pound, or face to blanch.
To eye the basilisk was not a risk:
No mortal perished from its evil stare.
Nor did the creatures at the well await
The unicorn to purify the spring.

92. The tiger, the fierce lion, and the panther
Were all as tame and indolent as bunnies,
While every timid beast appeared to be
Ferocious as a lion or a tiger.
Nor did these creatures flee the sight of man:
The birds—white, yellow, black, and red—did not
In those days hide in brush, but would alight
Upon a person's shoulders, head, or hand.

93. The cruel longing to devour flesh
Had not yet come into the human breast.
Such food as this has turned us into brutes,
Divesting us of all that makes us human.
From this, the war between mankind and beast.
From this, the bird's retreat from leaf to leaf

And her heartrending cries when she finds out
Her darling chicks are missing from the nest.

94. The piteous bleatings of a ewe who'd lost
     Her precious little lamb were never heard.
     No cow then filled the sky with groans on coming
     Home from the slaughterhouse without her calf.
     Nor were the wild beasts killed for having furs
     That helped protect their limbs from winter's cold.
     Their trails were always safe, for neither bird
     Nor beast was hunted down for sport or meat.

95. The singing birds took wing from bough to bough
     Without a care for net or deadly snare.
     The partridge found her chicks all there each time
     She called them or convened them for a count.
     The fish were not yet prey to nets or hooks
     Or other traps concealed beneath their food,
     And purple mollusks were not tricked with wiles,
     Nor did their lifeblood stain expensive cloth.

96. The squid with its one hundred tentacles
     Approached the moray eel without dismay,
     And never tried to wind itself around
     The lobster's pair of mouths, which never bit
     Into the moray eel's defenseless spine:
     None sought to hurt the other for revenge.
     Today, each kind defeats the other, then
     Goes down to one that lost the previous round.

97. Just so, resplendent Day who after great
     Exertions chases rosy Dawn away;
     Then Dawn disperses Night who, though she flees,
     Is destined in the end to vanquish Day;
     Yet even as the hunter sounds her horn,
     She yields to Dawn in time's eternal round.
     The same befalls the creatures of the sea,
     If one must hazard an analogy.

98. The earth still hid within her bowels and depths
    The baneful lodes of every kind of ore.
    Fierce lust for gold had not yet gripped our hearts,
    And gold, for fear of us, had not turned yellow.
    No iron fit for war could be attained.
    No horses clinked with metal shoes or bits.
    No bronze prolonged the memory of the past,
    And no one thirsted after worldly fame.

99. Not yet had peaceful Nereus or any
    Daughter of his beheld or marveled at
    The shadow of the Argo in their realm,
    Or ships that move by means of wind or oar
    And measure off the miles of coast or sea,
    Using a thousand harmful new techniques.
    The word for island hadn't yet been heard:
    The world, it seems, was bounded by the shore.

100. Neither locale nor season changed the time
    Of year when flowers, leaves, and fruits appeared,
    And everywhere did nature spawn each kind
    Of creature, land, marine, or of the air.
    Each thing, when it was called by name, replied
    According to its natural faculties.
    No creature, then, was either old or young,
    Nor were there freaks of nature to be found.

101. The human body was so well disposed,
    The humors were so justly parceled out,
    That longing was restrained and well behaved.
    And none knew sorrow, anger, hope, or envy.
    Nature then roused an appetite that could
    Be satisfied by modest means: no moles
    Or growths defaced the skin, and none grew fat
    From eating too much food or things too sweet.

102. Robust and comely, sound and clean, men felt
    No cold or heat, for these did not exist.
    They did not flee from frost or leaky roofs,

Nor did Jove's lightning cause their hearts to quake.
And once the sun forsook the sky, they found
The sweetest slumber in their grassy beds.
When sunshine cleared the skies of morning fog,
And beasts and blossoms woke, they too arose.

103. Their ardent love was free of suffering,
      Nor were they plagued by jealousy or hope.
      Since it was always in conformity
      With God's and nature's will, their love was perfect,
      And with their sort of temperament, they roamed
      Alone but happy through the countryside.
      Their age was never either young or old.
      Their clothes were leaves, and flowers wreathed their brows.

104. What purple cloth could match these natural colors?
      What red or crimson dyed in wool or silk?
      What's gold or silver to a flower's hue?
      And so they led a life of endless joy.
      Oh that sweet season of most gentle love!
      Oh life of ceaseless longing, yet content,
      Where burning passion never stung, and love,
      Though consummated, did not breed fatigue.

105. Desire matched what nature's will decreed:
      It did not spurn, but relished what it had,
      And never grieved from what it owned or lacked.
      Desire never lessened or increased.
      It always liked the things it liked at first
      And never tired out or felt remorse.
      It satisfied itself, or else held back,
      But either way, it never suffered pain.

106. And every urge that might hurt others slept,
      Nor did ambition rise in any realm.
      In those days harmony prevailed between
      Contented man and heaven's constellations.
      Both mind and eye could see these lofty forms,
      Could see their virtues and their properties.

Thinking did not beget fatigue or doubt:
Without confusion man received the truth.

107.   The intellect then tallied with desire,
        The will with all the powers of our mind,
        And man was satisfied in knowing well
        That part of God his soul could comprehend.
        The foolish arrogance of erring minds
        To raise themselves on high did not exist:
        There was no search, beset by futile cares,
        For causes nature has concealed from us.

108.   Today, however, reason postulates
        A hidden good that it must seek. Desire
        Propels our puny minds to search, without
        Success: we rage, we grieve because the mind
        Has been too grand in dreaming up this good,
        But when it fails, we see that it can't see—
        We grieve that it's too small and would prefer
        To be stone blind than not see perfectly.

109.   Though Truth's too much for it, it won't take less,
        But knowing less, it then presumes there's more.
        The mind, like fire set in wood that's green,
        Casts forth no light but fills the eyes with smoke.
        Nocturnal birds who seek the sun end up
        As laughingstocks; and Icarus, if he
        Ascends too high, must lose his wondrous plumes
        And tarry in the sky, a wingless bird.

110.   A migratory bird that due to cold
        Has given up her native shore to cross
        The sea, soon wearies, sinking to the waves,
        And seeing that there's only water, grieves.
        No bough or reef's in sight to stay her flight,
        Yet if she spies some boat that plows the main,
        She fears the hands of man no less than storms
        At sea, and doubtful, stays among the waves.

111.   Thus if the mind deserts its place of birth
         It throws itself in disarray. In quest
         Of unknown shores, it too will end up in
         The waves, exhausted and confused. In those
         Days, though, the nimble mind beheld a truth
         That suited its capacities, nor did
         Presumption spoil this good: men liked just what
         They had, and what they understood sufficed.

112.   What God and nature brought to light about
         Themselves, they grasped without fatigue or doubt.
         No foolish, anxious quibbling provoked
         Their bile or fostered overheated blood.
         The naked truth, magnanimous and pure,
         Did not exact long sleepless nights of study:
         Once having seen her true, sweet loveliness,
         The mind, fulfilled, requested nothing more.

113.   Prometheus, who longed to know too much,
         Divested man of his true happiness,
         And brought an end to this auspicious age.
         Thus too much knowing causes misery.
         His foolish brother, knowing far too little,
         Released into the world disease and death.
         Too little knowing or too much brings grief,
         For each is equidistant from the mean.

A Wood of Love II (selections)

Written between 1486 and Lorenzo's death in 1492, the second "Wood of Love" has 142 stanzas and is, as far as I know, the first classical *silva* in Italian. As in the "Corinto" and the "Ambra," Lorenzo makes brilliant use of classical myth, but here he joins myth to a more complex, in this case, Platonic conception of love. The second "Wood of Love," which actually should precede the shorter, first "Wood of Love" (see Castagnola lxxxvii–lxxxviii), is at once one of Lorenzo's most fascinating and difficult works. Through what at first seems a discontinuous series of images (Spring), personifications (Jealousy, Hope), and myths (the Golden Age), Lorenzo explores the inner drama of love, its pathologies and splendors. In the guise of longing for his absent lady, the poet's persona is actually searching for his own soul or anima.

The classical *silva* was a sort of grab-bag poem whose heterogeneous contents were brought together through juxtaposition by the poet-*bricoleur*. While Lorenzo's poem retains some of this character, recent critics have demonstrated the fundamental unity and coherence of the work (see Sturm 112–16 and Castagnola lxxiv–lxxxi).

Unfortunately, lack of time prevented me from translating the entire poem. The sections included do reflect, however, Lorenzo's vigorous, original reworking of classical materials. In the myth of the golden age, for instance, we are given a virtual bestiary of paradisal fauna. More significant, Lorenzo uses the golden age to show how human desire, belief, and knowing might otherwise have been constituted, and thereby illuminates the nature of these functions as they really are (see Levin 41–42).

For other interpretations of the "Wood of Love," see Martelli 1965a, 135–78, and Orvieto 1976, 54–59.

I have consulted the standard text in Bigi 1965 but mainly have followed Castagnola's superb critical edition (1986). In the translation of the title, however, I have retained the traditional form found in Bigi.

20.1.	*And you will see, as if it were in spring*: the beloved's illuminating presence will be like spring to the lover. She, like the new, vigorous sun, will cause spring to return.
25.1.	*Flora*: goddess of flowers.
25.3.	*Zephyr*: the gentle west wind of spring.
26.1.	*Clytie will leave her ancient lover*: Clytie is a kind of sunflower or heliotrope whose flower always faces the sun. She was once a nymph who loved the sun, *her ancient lover*, but he spurned her.
26.3.	*Toward this new ardent rising*: that is, toward the poet's lady, whose presence is more powerful than the sun's.
26.7–8.	The rays from the lady's eyes, rather than those of the sun, will cause the dew to evaporate.
27.7.	*Nereus*: a god of the sea, whose daughters are the Nereids.
40.2.	*Amor*: the god Eros or love.
40.6.	*the shadow realm*: Hades, the realm of the dead, ruled by Pluto and inhabited by the avenging spirits, the Furies.

40.8.   *the Age of Gold*: Saturn, the father of Jove, presided over the Age of Gold, a paradisal period of human history. See stanzas 84–113 below.

41.4.   *her*: i.e., Jealousy.

42.3.   *Seductive son*: i.e., Amor.

44.8.   *Tartarus*: Hades.

45.6.   *Cerberus*: mythical three-headed dog who guards Hades.

71.7.   *Minerva*: goddess of wisdom whose magical shield allows her to see Hope's face.

73.1.   *Pluto*: i.e., the realm of Hades.

73.3.   *Juno*: goddess wife of Jove; she governs the weather.

73.5.   *Vulcan*: god of fire, volcanoes, and metalworking.

73.8.   *Iris*: the rainbow.

84.1.   *Prometheus*: i.e., Forethought, the Titan who stole fire from the gods and gave it to man, thus helping to bring the Golden Age to an end.

84.4.   *the Golden Age*: mythical age of peace and harmony before the introduction of fire and the various plagues and vices introduced through Prometheus's brother Epimetheus and Pandora.

91.5   *the basilisk*: mythical, dragonlike monster whose glance was fatal.

91.7–8.   Unicorns were thought to be able to purify tainted springs by touching the waters with their horns.

96.7–8.   These lines mean that such combat is foolish, for whoever wins will be defeated in the next round.

97.5.   *the hunter*: i.e., Night.

99.3.   *the Argo*: ship of the legendary Argonauts, here considered the first ship to sail the seas.

109.6.   *Icarus*: he flew too close to the sun, which melted the wax of his manmade wings, causing him to plunge to his death.

113.5.   *His foolish brother*: Epimetheus (Afterthought) neglected Prometheus's advice to refuse gifts from the gods. He married Pandora, the first woman and a gift to him from the gods. The ills and plagues of the world came when she let them out of the jar or box that was her dowry.

Carnival and Dance Songs

Dance Song

Oh lovely women, months I've passed
   In hunting for my heart.
My thanks to you, Love, for your part
   In finding it at last.

She dances in this dance perhaps,
   Who stole my heart away,
And has it still, and ever will,
   Up to my dying day.
So kind is she and virtuous,
   She'll always have my heart.
My thanks to you, Love, for your part
   In finding it at last.

Oh lovely women, here is how
   I found my heart again:
After I felt it fly from me
   I searched all over, when
I spied two pretty eyes, and there,
   In hiding, was my heart.
My thanks to you, Love, for your part
   In finding it at last.

What penance does this thief deserve
   Who thus my heart did snare?
Yet how her face shows love! How graceful
   She appears, how fair!
So let her heart stay fettered, ever
   Burning with my heart.

My thanks to you, Love, for your part
   In finding it at last.

Oh Love, tie up this bandit, burn her
   With her stolen prize!
If she entreats you, close your ears,
   Don't look her in the eyes!
But if you've darts and arrows, use them
   To avenge my heart.
My thanks to you, Love, for your part
   In finding it at last.

Song of the Village Lasses

Alas, it's in this Carnival
That we have lost, oh ladies dear,
Our husbands, and without them we're
Not doing well, not well at all.

The six of us are from Narcetri—
Our work is cultivating fields:
We gather certain lovely fruits
The countryside around us yields.
If one of you is so courteous
To tell us where our husbands are,
You'll have these fruits as gifts from us.
   They're sweet, and they will do no harm at all.

Cucumbers, large ones, we have brought,
All rough outside and strange to view.
It seems they're full of warts, but then
They're laxative and wholesome too.
First take the fruit in hand. Expose
The core by pulling back the skin.
Open your mouth and suck. For those
   Who know the way, it does not hurt at all.

Among these fruits there is a melon,
As big as any gourd you know.
We save it for its seeds so that
From it a multitude can grow.
The seeds will make the tongue turn red
From stem to tip. It's like a dragon—
Handsome and inspiring dread,
    A terror that will do no harm at all.

We also have some beanpods, long
And tender, morsels for a pig.
We have still others of this kind,
But they're well cooked, quite firm, and big,
And each will make a foolish clown
If you first take the tail in hand
Then rub it gently up and down.
    He threatens, but will do no harm at all.

Such fruits are eaten after dinner,
A way now held in high regard.
This seems to us all wrong: digesting
Them then is really very hard.
Once nature's full, one shouldn't start
Again; but do it as you will,
Before, or in the after part:
    Before, however, doesn't hurt at all.

And we'll bestow on you these fruits
Such as they are, and that's the truth
(Just tell us where our husbands lurk)
For we're still in the bloom of youth.
But if you're ingrates or too proud,
We'll find some other means so that
Our land does not remain unplowed.
    We long to join in Carnival!

Song of the Cicadas

The damsels begin:

Women are we, as you can see,
Young, delectable, and gay.

We're going forth to pleasure all,
As is the law of Carnival.
Cicadas and the envious
Are vexed at others' happiness:
They find release in calumny,
These cicadas that you see.

We are unlucky, there's no doubt!
Not just in summer but throughout
The year cicadas prate away,
And ever seek us out as prey.
But they are vile themselves, you see,
Who speak of others viciously.

The cicadas reply:

We only do, oh pretty creatures,
That which is proper to our natures.
It's you, though, who're the guilty ones
Each time you fail to curb your tongues:
Do what you may, but learn at least
To hide it from the light of day!

Who acts now and doesn't dawdle
Escapes the risk of idle twaddle.
If they must perish, what's the sense
Of keeping lovers in suspense?
So if you hate what tattlers say,
Go and do it, while you may.

The damsels reply:

What good will be our loveliness
If as we chatter it grows less.
Long live love and gentle manners!
Death to envy and to slanders!
Talk, then, you who love hearsay:
While you prattle, we will play!

Song of the Seven Planets

We the Seven Planets leave
    Our noble residence on high
That we may make your world perceive
    The powers of the starry sky.

From us proceed all earthly goods and woes,
Whatever brings you pain or consolation:
All that befalls a man, a beast, a rose,
Or stone must have in us its derivation.
We conquer all who dare our will oppose,
    But gently guide each person who complies.

Misers and wretches, subtle cunning knaves,
Rich men and prelates, men of high degree,
The hot and rash, the barbarous and brave,
Renowned musicians, scholars, royalty,
And smooth-tongued talkers, liars, the depraved:
    Each mode of human life from us derives.

Venus, so gracious, elegant, and bright,
Impels the heart to love and gentleness:
Who touches the sweet fire of her light
Will always long for someone's loveliness.
The birds and beasts know well this sweet delight,
    And by this means your mortal world survives.

So come, let's follow this propitious star,
Oh lovely maids, oh lads of goodly measure!
The graceful Cyprian summons you to her
That you may spend your days in mirth and pleasure.
Nor think that this sweet season will recur:
    Our time is lost forever when it flies.

Now the sweet season bids us to refrain
From melancholy thoughts and vain laments.
And while some days of short-lived life remain,
Let's give ourselves to love and merriments.
Find pleasure you who can, for wealth and fame
    Are worthless things to those with joyless lives.

The Triumph of Bacchus and Ariadne

How lovely is youth in its allure,
Which ever swiftly flies away!
Let all who want to, now be gay:
About tomorrow no one's sure.

Here are Bacchus, Ariadne,
For one another all afire:
Because time flies and plays us false,
They always yield to their desire.
These nymphs of theirs and other folk
Are merry every single day.
Let all who want to, now be gay:
About tomorrow no one's sure.

Those who love these pretty nymphs
Are little satyrs, free of cares,
Who in the grottoes and the glades
Have laid for them a hundred snares.
By Bacchus warmed and now aroused
They skip and dance the time away.

Let all who want to, now be gay:
About tomorrow no one's sure.

These nymphs fall gladly for the ruses
That the satyrs execute:
Who can avoid the lure of Love
Except some rude, unfeeling brute?
So now among themselves they mingle,
Playing and singing all the day.
Let all who want to, now be gay:
About tomorrow no one's sure.

Behind the rest, that heavy sack
Astride a jackass is Silenus,
Old and drunk and ever jocund,
Long on years but not on leanness.
Although he cannot sit up straight,
He's full of cheer and laughs away.
Let all who want to, now be gay:
About tomorrow no one's sure.

And last of all appears King Midas:
All that he touches turns to gold.
But if it does not make him happy,
What is the use of wealth untold?
What sweetness will he ever taste
Who has a thirst he can't allay?
Let all who want to, now be gay:
About tomorrow no one's sure.

Now listen well to what I say,
That none may count on what's to come.
Let men and women, young and old,
Today be glad and have some fun.
Let's cast aside all gloomy thoughts
And have perpetual holiday.
Let all who want to, now be gay:
About tomorrow no one's sure.

Among you lasses and young lovers
Long live Bacchus and Desire!
Now let us pipe and dance and sing,
Our hearts consumed with sweetest fire!
Away with suffering and sorrow!
Let what is fated have its way.
Let all who want to, now be gay:
About tomorrow no one's sure.

Carnival and Dance Songs

Lorenzo's dance and carnival songs are perhaps the most engaging of his lyric poems. Both kinds were meant to be sung, but unfortunately only a few of the musical settings remain. The carnival songs, as the name suggests, were performed in the pre-Lenten feast of Carnival, which probably had its roots in the ancient Roman Saturnalia. They invariably deal with love, and the treatment may be bawdy, as in the "Song of the Village Lasses," or more delicate, as in the "Song of the Cicadas." Men in masks and costumes, representing the various trades or mythological or allegorical figures, were pulled through the streets on decorated wagons or floats on which they sang and enacted the songs. The floats for the mythological scenes were called Triumphs (*trionfi*). Hence the "Triumph of Bacchus and Ariadne," Lorenzo's most famous poem, considered by many the finest lyric of the Quattrocento.

Lorenzo wrote dozens of dance and carnival songs, the earliest of the dance songs going back to 1467 (Bigi 1965, 209). He composed the carnival songs, it seems, in the last decade of his life. The particular form as we know it, and perhaps the genre itself, was Lorenzo's invention (Bigi 1965, 231–32). The last three carnival songs in this selection date from 1489–90 (see Martelli 1965a, 37–51).

See also Orvieto 1976, 68–77, and for excellent commentaries on the songs included here, Sturm 77–85.

No authoritative edition of these songs exists. I have consulted the texts in Bigi 1965 and Simioni. Chastel's French translations were often helpful.

"Song of the Cicadas." The *cicadas* are spiteful gossips who are jealous of the damsels' success in love.

"Song of the Seven Planets." *The powers of the starry sky* refer to the astrological influences of the planets on human life. In the fifth stanza the *graceful Cyprian* is Venus, goddess of love.

"The Triumph of Bacchus and Ariadne." *Bacchus* is the Greek god of wine. According to one tradition, he discovered and married *Ariadne*, the beautiful daughter of King Minos of Crete, after she had been abandoned by Theseus on the island of Naxos. In the fifth stanza *Silenus* is the fat, satyrlike companion of Bacchus. *King Midas* (stanza 6) found his life miserable after Bacchus granted his wish that all he touch turn to gold.

Letters

Translated by Janet Ross and Jon Thiem

1. To his father Piero de' Medici at Florence
Pistoia, 24 July 1463

Magnifice vir pater, etc. With God's mercy and help we arrived here safely yesterday evening around 11:00 P.M., and we dismounted at the Bishop's Palace, where we have been very well received, likewise by all the people here. And because we are in the middle of a feast day and are eager to see what lies on the road further ahead, we would be happy, insofar as it pleases Your Magnificence, to go Wednesday morning to see Lucca, and then we would like to go on to Pisa to visit and inspect our properties; from there we will leave very early, to return home and to you. We urgently beg you, then, to be agreeably disposed to this recreation of ours, and grant us your permission. To obtain it from you, we are sending this very servant, through whom may it please you to write us that this is agreeable to you. And if you do not reply, we will interpret your lack of an answer as a quick way of giving your consent. And so, as ever, we commend ourselves to Your Magnificence. May God most high preserve your happiness.

> Pistoia, the 24th of July 1463,
> your sons, Lorenzo de' Medici
> Braccio Martelli
> Sigismondo della Stufa
> Francesco the Notary

P.S. We were hoping to be able to send you some trout, but because it rained so furiously last Friday, the waters swelled up and few fish were caught. But to make up for the trout we are sending the Magnificent Giuliano a piece of veal, which we hope he will gladly accept.

2. To his mother Lucrezia at Bagno a Morba
Florence, 19 September 1467

I thought I should have been with you by now, but the weather has become much cooler, and Maestro Mariotti does not think it would be good for my eczema to return there. Therefore I have determined not to come. Piero has promised to go and see you either with Messer Benedetto or soon afterwards. Let us find that you are so improved in health that nothing more will be necessary. We are all well here, particularly Piero, whose only need is to hear oftener about you; in truth, whether from the negligence of the writer or perhaps of the messenger, till now we have had but scant news. Therefore to satisfy us all, more particularly Piero, see that we get your answers more quickly, and apply yourself diligently to benefit from your sojourn there. I commend myself to you.—In Florence on the 19th day of September 1467,

Your Lorenzo de' Medici

P.S. I should be glad if you send me back my purple cioppetta (tunic) as I have nothing to wear; the other things I do not need for now.

3. To his wife Clarice at Florence
Milan, 22 July 1469

I have arrived here safely and am well. I am sure this will please you more than any other news save that of my return, judging by my own feelings of longing for you and for home. Make much of Piero, Mona Contessina, and Mona Lucrezia. I shall hasten to finish here and return to you, for it seems to me a thousand years since I saw you. Pray to God for me, and if you want anything from here let me know, so long as I have not already left. From Milan, July 22, 1469.

Your Lorenzo de' Medici

4. To Bona and Gian Galeazzo Maria Sforza,
Dukes of Milan
Florence, 26 April 1478

My most illustrious Lords. Just now my brother Giuliano was killed, and I am in utmost danger of losing my control of the state. Therefore, my Lords, now is the time to help your servant Lorenzo. Send as many people as you can with the greatest haste, so that they can be the shield and health of my regime, as they have always been.

In Florence, 26 of April 1478

Your servant Lorenzo de' Medici

5. To Rene I of Anjou
Florence, 19 June 1478

Most Serene King and especially my Lord. The letter Your Majesty has deigned to write about our unhappy case, replete with great love and paternal benevolence, shows me how keenly you felt our misfortune, and how kindly disposed you are towards me. Should I even attempt to return adequate thanks to Your Majesty I should deserve to be called utterly unfit to understand so great a benefit, because words so full of love and benevolence coming from Your Majesty to a humble servant cannot be repaid by any act or word. I can therefore only beg Your Majesty specially to accept my heartfelt declaration of loyalty as a token and a pledge of my gratitude, trusting that God will repay to Your Majesty the rest of my debt. As to Your Majesty's wise counsels to bear this calamity with fortitude, you may rest assured that I do not so much deplore what has happened to myself as the grave affront to the Christian name; because where I hoped, in such bitter trouble, to receive help, I found instead the fountain-head and instigator of all ill. For he, in the presence of many, dared to confess spontaneously that this crime was caused by him, and promulgated against me, my children, successors, intimates, and well-wishers, an iniquitous sentence of excommunication. Not satisfied with that, he is arming against this Republic, has instigated King Ferdinand against us, and has urged the King's eldest son to march against us with a formidable army in order with violence and arms to destroy him he could not succeed in utterly ruining by deceit and fraud. For I well know, and God is my witness, that I have committed no crime against the Pope, save that I am alive, and having been protected by the grace of Almighty God have not allowed myself to be murdered. This is my sin, for this alone have I been excommunicated and massacred. But I believe that God, scrutinizer of hearts and most just Judge, who knows my innocence, will not permit this and will defend me, whom He saved from those sacrilegious hands in front of His Body, from such unjust calumny. On our side we have Canon Law, on our side laws natural and political, on our side truth and innocence, on our side God and men. He has violated all these at once, and now desires to annihilate us. I write these things to Your Majesty as to a compassionate father, and from you, on account of your goodness, piety, and greatness of soul, I have no doubt I shall receive much help, favour, and military aid, if required. For we cannot believe that any good man can tolerate that he, who wilfully precipitates himself into such an abyss of crime, should drag with him the Christian name. May Your Majesty keep well, to whom I humbly commend myself.—Florence, June 19, 1478.

6. To the Signoria of Florence
San Miniato, 7 December 1479

My Most Illustrious Lords. It is not from presumption that I did not notify the reason of my departure to Your Illustrious Excellencies, but because it seemed to me that the agitated and disturbed condition of our city demands acts and not words. I conceive that she desires, and indeed has extreme need of peace. Seeing that all other endeavors have been fruitless, I have determined to run some peril in my own person rather than expose the city to disaster. Therefore, with the permission of Your Excellencies of the Signoria, I have decided to go voluntarily to Naples. Being the one most hated and persecuted by our enemies, I may also, by placing myself in their hands, be the means of restoring peace to our city. One of two things is certain, either His Majesty the King loves our city as he has asserted and some have believed, and is attempting to gain our friendship by affronting us rather than by despoiling us of liberty; or His Majesty really desires the ruin of this Republic. If his intentions are good there is no better way of testing them than by placing myself voluntarily in his power, and I make bold to say that this is the only way to make peace and to advance, as much as possible, the condition of our city in this direction. If His Majesty the King intends indeed to attack our liberty it seems to me well to know the worst quickly, and that one should be injured rather than the many. I am most glad to be that one, for two reasons; first, because being the principal object of our enemies' hatred I can more easily and better find out the will of the King, as it may be that our enemies only seek to injure me. The other reason is that having a greater position and larger stake in our city, not only than I deserve but probably than any citizen in our days, I think that I am more bound than any other man to give up all to my country, even my life. These are the feelings with which I go, for perhaps our Lord God desires that this war, which began with the blood of my brother and my own, should be put an end to by me. My ardent wish is that either my life or my death, my misfortunes or my well-being, should contribute to the good of our city. I shall therefore carry out my idea. If it succeeds according to my wishes and hopes I shall be most glad to benefit my country at the risk of my life and at the same time to save myself. Should evil befall me I shall not complain if it benefits our city, as it certainly must; for if our adversaries only aim at me, they will have me in their hands: if they want anything else it will be plain to all. I am certain that our citizens will unite to protect their liberty, so that by the grace of God it will be defended as was always done by our fathers. I go full of hope, and with no other object than the good of the city, and I pray God to give me grace to perform what is the duty of every man towards his country. I commend myself humbly to Your Excellencies of the Signoria. From San Miniato on the 7th day of December 1479.

Lorenzo de' Medici.

7. To the Duke Ercole D'Este at Ferrara
Florence, 5 February 1486

Your Excellency has in your library a book by an historian named Dione, *de Romanis historiis*, which I have an extreme desire to see, both on account of the consolation I derive from history and also because my son Piero, who has some knowledge of Greek literature, has begged me to get this book for him to read, which I understand is very rare in Italy. Your Excellency can understand how grateful I shall be for the loan of it for a few days, and therefore I beg you to grant my request and with all eagerness I await the book. I commend myself to Your Excellency.—Florence, February 5, 1485 (1486). Your Excellency's servant,

Lorenzo de' Medici

8. To Pope Innocent VIII at Rome
Florence, 20 November 1488

My ambassador has written to tell me that at last by the kindness of

Your Holiness the contract of the alum works has been awarded to me; for this I owe infinite thanks to Your Holiness who has thus added another to the many obligations I already owe, and hope to enjoy in the future from the liberality and kindness of Your Holiness. I am exceedingly grateful for and pleased by the paternal charity shown to me every day by Your Holiness, and should be yet more happy did I not hear that Your Holiness has been suffering from gout and slight fever. Although the attack is, by the grace of God, not a severe one, still, depending as I do on Your Holiness, and Your Holiness' life being of such importance, I cannot but feel uneasy even at a small indisposition, particularly as these attacks come oftener than one could wish. Your Holiness can rest assured that even as S. Francis by reason of his stigmate felt the pain of the wounds of Jesus Christ, thus do I feel every pain and ill suffered by Your Holiness in my own person and am much vexed thereby. Among other things the condition of our Ser Francesco touches me deeply, as well as that of other dependents of Your Holiness, who by reason of the uprightness and honesty of Your Beatitude may be said to be still fasting and to have had but a small share of the great good fortune which our Lord God has so worthily bestowed on Your Holiness. Should anything happen to Your Holiness, *quod absit*, the sepulchre will open also for them in that same hour. Although I feel compassion for them all I am more moved by what ought to touch Your Holiness more nearly than myself, and that is the sad condition of poor Ser Francesco, who in the five years of the pontificate of Your Holiness has never yet had anything he can call his own. Your Holiness is the best judge of what support he enjoys in the Sacred College and what office, dignity or means, he has to enable him to live, even poorly. If Your Holiness considers the lives of other Popes you will see that there are but few who, after five years of pontifical rule, and some in even less time, have not begun to want to act like Popes [i.e., prodigally], and have not shown the respect for honesty and uprightness displayed by Your Holiness, which is by now justified before God and man. But speaking as a devoted servant, this honesty might now be imputed and attributed to another motive. Maybe I appear presumptuous, but zeal and the duty I owe to Your Holiness so touch my conscience that I must speak thus openly and remind Your Holiness that all men are mortal, and that a Pope is what he wills to be; he cannot leave the Papacy as an inheritance and can only call his own the honours, the glory and the benefits, he gives to his family. The prudence, experience and long acquaintance Your Holiness has of the papal court, will I am sure without words from me, recall to Your Holiness what always happens to the fortune and inheritance of popes, and seeing that Ser Francesco and the others of Your Holiness' family are as yet not to be envied but rather merit compassion, Your Sanctity ought to follow the example of Your Holiness' predecessors and place them in such a position that they should have as little need of others as is possible, particularly as whatever is bestowed on them does not diminish the substance of Your Holiness and is not lost or thrown away. Briefly, with all humility, I entreat Your Sanctity at last to begin and act as a Pope with regard to the family of Your Holiness and not to trust so much in posterity and good health, which can only retard the fulfilment of what Your Holiness intends to do for them. Delay might perhaps prevent this being accomplished. Especially do I recommend Your and my Ser Francesco and the Lady Maddalena, who pray that God may grant Your Holiness a long life in order that their affairs may be properly adjusted, and when better arranged they will give thanks to God and to Your Holiness and have reason to remember and to bless the day when Your Sanctity was called to the honours and dignity of the pontificate. It is time, Holy Father, to liberate these Holy Fathers from limbo, so that it may not happen to them as to the Jews who awaited the Messiah. I beg Your Holiness' pardon with all humility and reverence for this my presumption only caused by reasons which I am sure Your Holiness will appreciate, and I place myself humbly at Your most holy feet. Humilis Servitor,

Lorenzo de' Medici

9. To Giovanni Lanfredini, Florentine Ambassador at Rome
Florence, October 1489

To my great vexation, I hear how this work of Mirandola's is abused, and were I not sure that such persecution is dictated solely by envy and malignity, by my faith, I should not mention it. The book has been examined by all the most learned priests here and well-known men of saintly life and good reputation. It has been highly approved of by them as a Christian and a marvellous work. I am not so bad a Christian as to remain silent or to encourage him if I thought otherwise. I am certain that if he recited the Credo those spiteful men would say it was heresy. If His Holiness had the intelligence to understand this and was not too busy, I am sure these accusations would fall to the ground and truth would prevail; but he is obliged to trust to others. This poor man is unable to defend himself because they say the arguments he puts forth are against His Holiness. If he had to contend with them only, without the authority of the Pope to back them, I am sure he would soon silence them. It is his misfortune to have to submit to the judgment of ignorant and malicious men who use the Pope as a shield. I have already told you that I believe all this is done with the intent to drive him to despair and cause him to lose his head so that eventually he should turn against the Pope; for believe me, Giovanni, he is one who could commit either great evil or great good. His life and habits demonstrate this. If they drive him into another path I shall lose little, as I know that wherever he may be he will always bear me goodwill because of my great affection for him. I have never been able to make you understand this; and without entering into details, which I cannot do, I must tell you he has been sorely tempted to do something which might raise a great scandal, and I have always stopped him. Lately he has been leading a saintly life here, and his mind is at rest. These devils with their persecutions will tempt him. People place far too much faith in them. In short I can only grieve over all this and beg you again to use all your cleverness in order to arrange matters, for you have no idea how it vexes and irritates me. If you knew how much, you would never rest until you have taken it off my mind.—October 1489.

10. To Giovanni Lanfredini, Florentine Ambassador at Rome
Florence, 17 October 1489

By your letter of the 13th I understand that the Pope has taken umbrage at the petition, transmitted by you, that he not proceed further with these denunciations. Anything that vexes His Sanctity annoys me, and I should be very sorry if he thought that any act or word of mine was not dictated by a desire for the good of His Holiness. You can assure him that in every decision and action I am always his true servant and shall ever be. If I advised moderation in these proceedings against the King [of Naples] I only did so for the reasons that follow. As I wrote the other day, it seems to me necessary that His Holiness should decide on following one of three paths: enforce his will by war against the King, or come to some agreement, or, if an honourable agreement is not possible, at the present, to temporize in a dignified way, and wait for a better occasion. The first would be the most honourable, but I conceive it to be dangerous and very costly; nor do I think it possible to achieve this now without putting a new ruler over the Kingdom of Naples. For this, according to my views, three things are necessary: either Venice or Milan must be a party to the enterprise; second, the new ruler must be strong and well supplied with men and money; and third, the Holy Father must make every possible effort without stint of money or other things, to carry the thing through. It is indispensable that the Pope and the new ruler, whoever he may be, should be stronger than the King alone, supposing always that Venice adheres to this plan and would prevent Milan from helping the King. If they were to have an understanding with the Neapolitan Barons, or other such supporters, they could accomplish this much more easily. I may have been mistaken as to the first proposition when I dissuaded His Holiness from following it, but the preconditions for this did not seem to me sufficient. Perhaps I am not enough versed in all the secrets. From what I see or understand there is no reason that His Holiness should at the present time have this plan or hope, for either Spain or France must be made to intervene to achieve this purpose. Spain does not appear to me strong enough, particularly as regards money. What reliance is to be placed on France, seeing the French nature, I know not. Supposing she changed her nature, I should agree with our Holy Father that it would be the best solution, for there would be less danger in augmenting the power of one of the house of Lorraine than of Spain, for the Duke of Lorraine is not King of France and we see by experience that the King of Naples is far more close to Spain than the Duke of Lorraine is to France. It is true that the Kings of Naples and Spain are not friends, and that whoever is King of Naples would act independently. For all these reasons, although there may be others I do not understand, I could never advise the Pope to undertake such an enterprise now; and in that case it does not help to exasperate the King with accusations and other threats. Even were His Holiness fully prepared to go forward I think he ought to avoid, all the more, the slightest sign of ill-will, in order not to incur any danger from what the King might do between threat and attack. This danger seems to me great. Therefore he would do better to dissimulate and make secret preparations, than to show anger before being ready to strike, which would only give an opportunity to others to make ready and to attack. So for every reason concerning this first course of action I do not think it wise to denounce the King. As to the second, concerning an agreement, I may also be mistaken, because conditions may have been proposed of which I am not aware, and which may be facilitated by this kind of denunciation, if the negotiations are advanced and nearly finished. In such a case showing a strong hand usually helps in coming to a resolution. But if there is nothing more than I know, the dealings seem bitter and not ready for an easy resolution; therefore such methods of negotiation might lead to a scandal or even to an open rupture, instead of to an agreement. The advantages of temporizing cannot, I think, be denied. There can be no doubt that it is better to maintain things as they are, preserving the reputation of His Holiness, than to tempt fortune; for you know better than I do that the King can do much harm. But, as I said before, I do not know enough about these matters so I cannot say more. If the Pope has good reasons for his fearless attitude let me know them also, to relieve my mind, for though not of a timid nature I am far more anxious about his affairs than about my own, because of the trust he reposes in me. If His Holiness is certain of his course, I have such faith in his prudence and authority that I too will rest easy. But until I hear these reasons for his confidence, I confess that I am uneasy. For the love of God let me know, as I usually do not feel well. The Pope must not on any account imagine that I think, do, or act, in any way against his interest, for the benefits I have received from His Holiness, and those I hope for, derive from his power and reputation. My opinion of the Lord Lodovico I have expressed, and have said what I thought of his character. My intentions are loyal, and as I depend much on His Holiness I can only repeat that if he can come to an honourable understanding with the King, a common agreement would be, I think, better than a good war. If there is any difficulty about this I would do my utmost to temporize, while preserving honour and security, supposing always that the above-mentioned conditions, of which I know nothing, and which would make it possible to act against the King, are non-existent. If they do exist I am sure the King would consent to honourable terms. Because I think the King may well find out what evil might befall him, I fear he might therefore become stronger. But all my suppositions are useless if the Pope has secret information unknown to me. I do not think this discourse of mine can offend His Holiness, when I add this proviso: I always intend to support that which will also be fortunate for His Holiness. I wish to be allowed to say what I think, but will act according to the wishes of our Holy Father. Thank him most heartily for the loving and kindly reply about protection of the Servite Order with regard to Messer Giovanni. For all these things I am forever indebted to His Holiness. I am very glad you have been to Cervetri and S. Severa, and most pleased that you were satisfied with the way Signor Francesco [Cybo] treats his subjects. God knows his honour and well-being are as dear to me as my own. I beg of you to do all you can to induce our Holy Father to bring to completion this affair of S. Severa. You see yourself the importance and the necessity of adding this state to that of Cervetri. I should also like to know about the affair of Gallese in order to reply to the friend who is coming here soon. It is urgent that His Holiness should once for all arrange the affairs of Signor Francesco so that I should not be daily worried about them, and that we can live in peace and harmony. To speak plainly, Signor Francesco does not have the position the nephew of a Pope ought to have, and yet we are now approaching the seventh year of the Pontificate. More regard should be shown to the increasing family, which is a valid reason for our Holy Father's aid. [. . .] Florence, October 17, 1489.

Lorenzo de' Medici

11. Instructions to his son, Cardinal Giovanni
Florence, March 1492

Messer Giovanni, you are much beholden to our Lord God, as we all are for your sake, for besides many benefits and honours our house has received from Him it has pleased Him to bestow on you the highest dignity our family has yet enjoyed. Great as this is, it is much enhanced by circumstances, particularly your youth and our condition. Therefore my first recommendation is that you endeavour to be grateful to our Lord God, remembering every hour that it is not by your own merits or solicitude that you have attained the Cardinalate, but by the wonderful grace of God. Show your gratitude to Him, justifying your position by leading a saintly, exemplary, and honest life. You are the more bound to do this because during your youth you have shown a disposition which gives hope of good fruit. It would be indeed most shameful, contrary to your duty, and to my expectations if at a time when others generally acquire more reason and a better understanding of life, you should forget the good precepts learned as a boy. It is incumbent on you to try and lighten the burden of the dignity you have attained by leading a life of good conduct and persevering in the studies suitable to your profession. I was greatly pleased last year to learn that without being reminded by anyone you had been several times to confession and to communion, for I conceive there is no better way of obtaining the grace of God than by habituating oneself to persevere in these duties. This seems to me the best advice I can begin with.

I know, as you are now going to Rome, that sink of all iniquities, that you will find some difficulty in following it, for bad examples are always catching, and inciters to vice will not be lacking. Your promotion to the Cardinalate, as you may imagine, at your age and for the other reasons already mentioned, will be viewed with great envy, and those who were not able to prevent your attaining this dignity will endeavour, little by little, to diminish it by lowering you in public estimation and causing you to slide into the same ditch into which they have themselves fallen, counting on success because of your youth. You must be all the firmer in your stand against these difficulties, as at present one sees such a lack of virtue in the College [of Cardinals]. I recollect however to have known a good many learned and good men in the College, leading exemplary lives. It will be well that you should follow their example, for by so doing you will be the more known and esteemed as being different from the others.

It is imperative above all things that you should avoid as you would Scylla and Charybdis the reputation of being a hypocrite and of evil fame. Be not ostentatious, and have a care to avoid anything offensive in conduct and in conversation, without affecting austerity or severity. These are things you will in time understand and practice better, I conceive, than I can write them. You know how important is the position and the example of a Cardinal, and that the world would be far better if the Cardinals were what they ought to be, for then there would always be a good Pope, from whom emanates, one may say, peace for all Christians. Make every effort therefore to be this; if others had done so we might hope for universal good. Nothing is more difficult than to hold converse with men of various characters, and in this I can ill advise you; only recollect when with the Cardinals and other men of rank to try and be charitable and respectful in your conversation, weighing your reasons well without being influenced by the passions of others; for many desiring what they cannot attain turn reason into abuse. Satisfy your conscience therefore by taking care that your conversation with every man should be devoid of insults. This seems to me a general rule most applicable in your case, for should passion by chance make someone into your enemy, as his enmity would have no reasonable cause, he may sometimes return with more ease to the old friendship. It will be better I think on this, your first visit to Rome, to use your ears more than your tongue.

Today I have given you entirely to our Lord God and to Holy Church; it is therefore essential that you become a good ecclesiastic, cherishing the honour and the State of the Holy Church and of the Apostolic See above anything else in this world, and devoting yourself entirely to their interests.

While doing this it will not be difficult for you to aid the city and our house, for the city being united to the Church, you must serve as the vital link, and our house will thus become part of the city. Although it is impossible to foresee what may happen, I think it is likely that a way will be found to save, as the proverb says, the goat and the cabbages, always keeping steadfastly to your above-mentioned duty of setting the interests of the Church above all else.

You are the youngest Cardinal, not only of the College, but the youngest that has hitherto been made; it is therefore most necessary that where you have to compete with the others you should be the most eager and the humblest, and avoid making others wait for you in Chapel, in Consistory, or in Deputation. You will soon learn who has a good or an evil reputation. With the latter avoid any great intimacy, not only on your own account, but for the sake of public opinion; converse in a general way with all. I advise you on feast-days to be rather below than above moderation, and would rather see a well-appointed stable and a well-ordered and clean staff of attendants than one that is pompous and richly attired. Let your life be regular and reduce your expenses gradually in the future, for the retinue and the master being both new, this will at first be difficult. Jewels and silken stuffs must be used sparingly by one in your position. Rather have a few good antiques and fine books, and well-bred and learned attendants, than many of them. Ask people to your own house oftener than you accept invitations to theirs but do both sparingly. Eat plain food and take much exercise, for those who wear your habit, if not careful, easily contract maladies. The rank of Cardinal is as secure as it is great; men therefore often become negligent; they conceive they have done enough and that without exertion they can preserve their position. This is often prejudicial to character and to life, and a thing against which you must guard; rather trust too little than too much in others. One rule I recommend to you above all others, and that is to get up early every morning; besides being good for the health one can meditate over and arrange all the business of the following day, and in your position, having to say the office, to study, to give audiences etc., you will find it most useful. Another thing absolutely necessary to one in your station is to reflect, particularly at this, the commencement of your career, in the evening on all you have to do next day, so that an unforeseen event may not come upon you unawares. As to speaking in the Consistory, I think it would be more seemly and becoming if you refer all that comes before you to His Holiness, alleging that as you are young and inexperienced you consider it your duty to submit everything to the most learned judgment of His Holiness. You will be asked, and with good reason, to intercede in various matters with our Holy Father. Be cautious however at the beginning to ask as few favours as possible and not to bother him; the disposition of the Pope is to be grateful to those who do not break his ears. Bear this in mind in order not to annoy him. When you see him, talk about amusing things, and if you have to beg, do it with all humility and modesty. This will please him and be in accordance with his nature. Keep well. Florence.

Letters

The notes follow the number of the particular letter. The translations of letters 1 and 4 are my own, and for them I have benefited from the texts and notes in *Lettere* I and III and Bigi 1965. Letters 2, 3, and 5 through 11 are the translations published by Janet Ross in 1911. They have been revised by me, partly on the basis of the texts and notes in *Lettere* I, III, and IV and Bigi 1965. The notes in Mutini 36–47 have been very helpful in revising letters 6, 8, and 10.

1. This letter by the teenaged Lorenzo and his friends gives us a glimpse of the "brigata" and its delight in excursions and fishing, etc. The letter complements "The Partridge Hunt," which Lorenzo probably wrote in the next year, and in which Sigismondo and Braccio are mentioned. Cf. also stanza 45 on fishing.

4. For the Pazzi conspiracy against the Medici, to which this letter is a response, see the Chronology, 1478, and Acton, passim. This urgent letter was sent on the very day Giuliano, Lorenzo's brother, was murdered.

5. The original is in Latin. The "fountain-head and instigator of all ill" is Pope Sixtus IV, who supported the Pazzi conspiracy and after its failure put Florence under interdict and encouraged military action against it.

6. Lorenzo's letter to the Signoria of Florence advising them of his visit to King Ferdinando of Aragon in Naples. See the Chronology, 1478–80.

8. Shortly after having received the lucrative alum monopoly from Pope Innocent VIII, Lorenzo pleads with him to give benefices to Fran-

ceschetto Cybo, the pope's son and Lorenzo's son-in-law. He frankly asserts that up to now the pope has been too honest and thrifty, if not miserly, and he compares the lot of his daughter and son-in-law to that of the Old Testament patriarchs in Limbo, awaiting deliverance.

9. Lorenzo intervenes on behalf of his brilliant young protégé Pico della Mirandola, a Neoplatonist philosopher whose books, including his most recent, *Heptaplus*, had raised charges of heresy against him by the theologians of papal Rome.

10. This letter was part of Lorenzo's successful effort to avert war between the papacy and Ferdinando of Aragon, King of Naples, a war that might have upset the balance of power in Italy, which Lorenzo had done so much to create, and that might have drawn foreign armies into Italy. Toward the end of the letter the pope's son and Lorenzo's son-in-law, Franceschetto Cybo, is referred to, euphemistically, as the pope's nephew (see also Letter 8). The last three sentences of the letter have to do with other matters and so have not been translated.

11. Written in the month before Lorenzo's death, for his son Giovanni, age sixteen, who was officially designated Cardinal on 9 March and shortly thereafter departed for Rome to be inducted into the College of Cardinals. Giovanni will later become Pope Leo X.

APPENDIX

Nencia of Barberino

1. I burn with love and feel compelled to sing
   About a lady who consumes my heart.
   Each time I hear her name my heart's aflutter,
   Whereupon I think that it may well desert
   Me utterly. In grace she has no peer,
   And from her eyes the flames of passion dart.
   I've been to town, I've also seen the city
   And yet I never saw a girl so pretty.

2. I've been in Empoli and to its market,
   And to the ones at Prato, San Casciano,
   Colle, Poggibonzi, San Donato,
   Grieve, and up here at Decomano;
   Markets at Castelfranco and Fegghine,
   At San Piero, Borgo, Gagliano;
   And yet the finest in creation is
   At Barberino, where my Nencia lives.

3. I never saw a lass so virtuous
   Or one brought up with such good sense as she.
   I never saw more shiny hair, a head
   More full of grace or shaped as beautifully,
   With eyes that light up like a festival
   Each time she raises them to look at me.
   Between's a pretty nose made with such skill
   It seems they bored the nostrils with a drill.

4. Her rosy lips appear to me as coral.
   And there behind them are her teeth—two rows—

More white than those of any horse, and on
Both sides she's more than twenty I'd suppose.
Her cheeks are white resembling finest crystal,
And ruddy in the middle like a rose—
All this without the help of rouge or cream,
A prettier thing you've surely never seen.

5. And so heartrending are those eyes of hers
That with them she could even pierce a wall.
And though her heart's as hard as cobblestone,
Whoever looks on her becomes her thrall.
A thousand lovers always follow her,
She whose eyes have captured one and all.
She turns and looks at every other swain;
To get a glimpse of her, I wrack my brain.

6. She's ruled me and so cut me down to size,
No longer can I use or wield my hoe;
I lack the strength to even swallow food,
The lass has tangled up my insides so.
I have become just like a web of knots,
And only through my love for her (although
I bear it fairly well) did she confound me
Who with a hundred plaited bonds has bound me.

7. Among a thousand beauties from the city
She is the one who'd be beyond compare,
And with her gentle words and graceful gestures
She always is superb, no matter where.
Her eyes are blacker than a piece of charcoal,
Beneath those tresses of her yellow hair,
The tips of which are curly all around,
And there, it seems, a thousand rings are bound.

8. She is indeed a ballerina, and like
A little goat she makes a leap or bound.
She whirls about just like a waterwheel
And slaps her little shoe that's left the ground.
And when she ends the dance she bows, then makes

Two little capers, once she's turned around:
She curtsies much more prettily, one warrants,
Than any woman living now in Florence.

9. My Nencia has no defects whatsoever:
   Her shape's ideal, her hue both red and white,
   The dimple in the middle of her chin
   Rounds off the lovely way she looks just right.
   Nor does she lack in sentiments. In her
   Has nature made the pattern of delight
   So fair, so graceful, and so beauteous,
   She plucks the heart away from most of us.

10. And you can easily call him fortunate,
    The one who marries such a pretty wife,
    And he who'll have that lily without leaves
    Can rightly praise the first day of his life.
    And he can well consider himself blessed
    Who has her ease his pain and inner strife,
    Who cradles in his arms a face like that
    So soft and white, and smooth as kidney fat.

11. My Nencia, if you only knew just how
    I love your eyes, the way they shine and glow,
    Or how much pain I feel, as if someone
    Were pulling out my teeth all in a row.
    If you could only know, your heart would burst,
    You'd leave the beaux you always have in tow
    And you would love alone Vallera true,
    Because his heart desires only you.

12. Nenciozza, you do make me waste away
    And yet this pleases you, you must admit.
    If only I could painlessly lay open
    My chest, I then would gladly cut a slit
    To show you that you're in my heart: I'd put
    It in your hand and make you look at it.
    Were you to cut it with a knife, don't doubt
    "Sweet Nencia" are the words it would cry out.

13. I always feel the need to be around you
     When with your friends I see you socialize,
     And then it seems my heart is plucked right out
     Each time I see another man make eyes
     At you. So deep inside my heart you've pierced,
     That I pour forth each day a thousand sighs,
     With little sobs and shining tears unchecked,
     Each one of which I send to you direct.

14. Last night I couldn't sleep at all—it seemed
     A thousand years before the night would fade,
     Before I'd lead my beasts outside and see
     Again your pretty face, oh lovely maid.
     Though it was dark, I had to leave my bed:
     I went beneath the bakehouse colonnade,
     Stood there an hour and a half, I bet,
     In the cool breeze, until the moon had set.

15. And when I saw you with your sheep, your dog
     Up front, go from the shed that's on your land,
     The tears began to well up in my eyes—
     More than a span I felt my heart expand.
     And then I drove my heifers and my calves,
     I drove them with my wooden staff in hand,
     Into a gully, with a lively stride,
     To wait for you, but you went back inside.

16. I next lay down along a stretch of stream
     And lolled about spread out across the grass,
     And there I waited more than half an hour
     Until your flock of lambs and sheep would pass.
     What keeps you in there that you don't come out?
     Come forth, ascend the alpine passes, lass,
     So though they're two of us, I'll have to run
     My beasts into your flock, and we'll be one.

17. My Nencia sweet, I plan to go to Florence
     To sell two loads of kindling Saturday,
     Kindling that I began to chop and split

While pasturing my heifers yesterday.
Just think of what you want that I can buy,
Some pretty bauble, anything you say:
Perhaps a sack of rouge, or facial cream,
Or needles, or some pins to tack a seam.

18.   Or else a necklace with some small red buttons
       And with a pendant—if you'd like to own
       One, like to wear it, I will look around:
       D'you want the buttons tiny or full blown?
       And if I have to cut them from the core
       Of my own shin or from some other bone,
       Or if I have to sell my shirt, don't fear,
       I'll get you what you want, my Nencia dear.

19.   Why don't you ask me for some toy? I'm sure
       You'd use some of the hundred kinds in stock:
       Some buckles, buttons, or some fancy hooks?
       Some lace to brighten up your dress or frock?
       Or do you want some ribbon for your bonnets,
       A little purse to decorate your smock?
       Or else, to tie your blouse around your waist
       A sash of pale blue silk—is that your taste?

20.   Sweet little lily mine, my herd nears home,
       So let me say a "fare thee well" for now.
       I'd hate it that from just my fiddling round
       There might get left in pasture calf or cow.
       I see my herd has crossed the stream at last,
       And Monna Masa calls me, anyhow.
       Stay happy, off I go to sing your fame—
       Nencia, my heart will always call your name.

Nencia of Barberino

The existence of four significantly different versions of "Nencia" (ranging from 12 to 51 stanzas) attests to the popularity of the work, the original

form of which probably antedates 1470. The poem is a delightful parody
of the pastoral lament (cf. "Corinto") and at the same time a travesty of
the conventions of the courtly love lyric (see stanzas 1, 3, 10, etc.). The
tone, the rustic analogies, and the Tuscan dialect expressions of the shep-
herd Vallera—the speaker, who is from the Mugello and in love with the
elusive Nencia—are humorously at odds with these conventions. Yet the
perennial appeal of the poem comes from the fact that Vallera, for all of
his goofy locutions, rises above caricature and engages the reader's sympa-
thies. "Nencia" helped inspire a new poetic genre ("versi nenciali") that
was much in vogue in the fifteenth and sixteenth centuries.

Serious doubts remain about the traditional attribution of the poem to
Lorenzo, and some evidence points to Bernardo Giambullari as the author.
For a history of the debates about the poem's authorship, see Bessi's intro-
duction to her critical edition of the various texts (1982).

This translation is based on the Volpi version in twenty stanzas, which is
reprinted in Bigi 1965, 129–35, and in Bessi 1982 (as Testo A). For fur-
ther commentary on the poem and its textual history, see Sturm 48–58,
Rochon 357–434, Orvieto 1976, 10–17, and Bessi 1982, passim.

1.1–8   The first six lines draw on the conventional diction of courtly love,
        but then the tone and word choice of the concluding couplet come
        as a jolt: they reveal that the speaker is no courtier but a common
        man of the people, a frequent visitor to the boisterous market
        towns around Florence (stanza 2). Cf. also the well-intentioned
        but comically ugly and inappropriate similes concluding stanzas 3
        and 10, and stanza 4, lines 1–4.

2.1–8   A list of Tuscan market towns. *Nencia* (line 8) is a diminutive of
        Lorenza, the feminine form of Lorenzo.

BIBLIOGRAPHY AND REFERENCES

Acton, Harold. 1979. *The Pazzi Conspiracy*. London: Thames and Hudson.

Allen, Michael J. B. 1975. *Marsilio Ficino: The Philebus Commentary*. Berkeley and Los Angeles: University of California Press.

Angeleri, C. 1942. "Magnifico Lorenzo." *La Rinascita* 24:225–32.

Bessi, Rossella, ed. 1982. *La Nencia da Barberino*. Rome: Salerno.

———, ed. 1986. *Ambra*. Florence: Sansoni Editore.

Bigi, Emilio. 1954. *Dal Petrarca al Leopardi*. Milan and Naples: Ricciardi.

———. 1961. *Letteratura italiana: i minori*. Vol. 1. Milan: Carl Marzorati.

———, ed. 1965. *Scritti scelti*. Turin: UTET.

———. 1967. *La cultura del Poliziano e altri studi umanistici*. Pisa: Nistri Lischi.

Boiardo, Matteo Maria. 1989. *Orlando Inamorato*. Trans. C. Ross. Berkeley and Los Angeles: University of California Press.

Bullard, Melissa Meriam. 1987. "The Magnificent Lorenzo de' Medici: Between Myth and History." In *Politics and Culture in Early Modern Europe*. Ed. P. Mack and M. C. Jacobs. Cambridge: Cambridge University Press.

Burke, Peter. 1972. *Culture and Society in Renaissance Italy, 1420–1540*. New York: Charles Scribner's Sons.

Bush, Douglas. 1963. *Mythology and the Renaissance Tradition in English Poetry*. New York: W. W. Norton.

Carducci, Giosue, ed. 1859. *Poesie*. Florence: Barbera.

Castagnola, Raffaella, ed. 1986. *Stanze*. Florence: Olschki.

Castaldo, A., ed. 1912. *Poesie*. Rome: Oreste Garroni.

Cavalli, G., ed. 1958. *Tutte le opere*. 3 vols. Milan: Rizzoli.

Chastel, André, trans. 1947. *Ambra. Chansons de Carnaval. L'Altercation*. Paris: La Colombe.

Chiari, Alberto. 1958. "Sul testo della laurenziana 'Uccellagione.'" *Rinascimento* 9:11–41.

Cloulas, Ivan. 1987. *Lorenzo il Magnifico*. Trans. C. Scarton. Rome: Salerno.

Condivi, Ascanio. 1976 (1553). *The Life of Michelangelo*. Trans. A. S. Wohl. Baton Rouge: Louisiana State University Press.

Cox-Rearick, Janet. 1984. *Dynasty and Destiny in Medici Art*. Princeton, N.J.: Princeton University Press.

Dacos, Nicole, ed. 1973. *Il tesoro di Lorenzo il Magnifico: Le gemme*. Florence: Sansoni.

De Lucchi, Lorna, trans. 1967 (1922). *An Anthology of Italian Poems*. New York: Biblo and Tannen.

De Robertis, Domenico. 1979. *L'esperienza poetica del Quattrocento*. Vol. 3 of *Storia della letteratura italiana*. Milan: Garzanti.

De Sanctis, Francesco. 1965 (1871). *Storia della letteratura italiana*. Florence: Sansoni.

Doglio, Federico, ed. 1987. *Rappresentazione di S. Giovanni e Paolo*. Rome: Coletti.

Eco, Umberto. 1989. *The Open Work*. Trans. A. Canogni. Cambridge, Mass.: Harvard University Press.

Elam, Caroline. 1988. "Art and Diplomacy in Renaissance Florence." *Journal of the Royal Society of Arts*: 813–25.

Ficino, Marsilio. 1985. *The Letters*. 3 vols. New York: Gingko Press.

Fletcher, Jefferson Butler. 1964 (1934). *Literature of the Italian Renaissance*. Port Washington, N.Y.: Kennikat Press.

Foster, P. E. 1978. *A Study of Lorenzo de' Medici's Villa at Poggio a Caiano*. 2 vols. New York: Garland.

Fryde, E. B. 1983. *Humanism and Renaissance Historiography*. London: Hambledon Press.

Gage, John. 1968. *Life in Italy at the Time of the Medici*. New York: G. P. Putnam's Sons.

Garin, Eugenio. 1972 (1963). *Portraits from the Quattrocento*. Trans. V. A. and E. Velen. New York: Harper and Row.

Gombrich, E. H. 1985. "The Early Medici as Patrons of Art." In *Norm and Form*. Chicago: University of Chicago Press.

Guicciardini, Francesco. 1966 (16th century). *History of Italy and History of Florence*. Trans. C. Grayson; ed. J. R. Hale. London: New English Library.

Hale, J. R. 1977. *Florence and the Medici: The Pattern of Control*. London: Thames and Hudson.

Hibbard, Howard. 1985. *Michelangelo*. New York: Harper and Row.

Hibbert, Christopher. 1985. *The Rise and Fall of the House of Medici*. Harmondsworth, Middlesex: Penguin Books.

Hook, Judith. 1984. *Lorenzo de' Medici: An Historical Biography*. London: Hamish Hamilton.

Jordan, Constance. 1986. *Pulci's* Morgante: *Poetry and History in Fifteenth-Century Florence*. Washington, D.C.: Folger Shakespeare Library.

Kennedy, William J. 1989. "Petrarchan Figurations of Death in Lorenzo de' Medici's Sonnets and *Comento*." In *Life and Death in Fifteenth-Century Florence*. Ed. M. Tetel et al. Durham, N.C.: Duke University Press.

Kristeller, Paul Oskar. 1956. "Lorenzo de' Medici platonico." In *Studies in Renaissance Thought and Letters*. Rome: Edizioni di Storia e Letteratura.

Langedijk, Karla. 1981–83. *The Portraits of the Medici*. 3 vols. Florence: Studio per Edizioni scelte.

Levin, Harry. 1969. *The Myth of the Golden Age in the Renaissance*. New York: Oxford University Press.

Lipari, Angelo. 1973 (1936). *The Dolce Stil Novo According to Lorenzo de' Medici*. New York: AMS Press.

McCarthy, Mary. 1959. *The Stones of Florence*. New York: Harcourt Brace Jovanovich.

Machiavelli, Niccolò. 1963 (1520–25). *Istorie Fiorentine*. In *Opere*. Milan: Riccardo Ricciardi.

Maier, Bruno. 1949. *Lettura critica del "Corinto" di Lorenzo de' Medici*. Trieste: Zigiotti.

———. 1954. *Classici italiani nella storia della critica*. Vol. 1. Ed. W. Binni. Florence: La Nuova Italia.

———, ed. 1969. *Opere scelte*. Novara: Istituto Geografico De Agostini.

Mallett, Michael. 1984. Review of J. Hook's *Lorenzo de' Medici*. *The Times Literary Supplement (17 August)*: 914.

Mangino, I. 1937. *Il "Simposio" o "I beoni" di Lorenzo de' Medici*. Naples: Ricciardi.

Marshall, Murray L., trans. 1949. *The Comment of Lorenzo de' Medici*. Washington, D.C.: The Marshalls.

Martelli, Mario. 1965a. *Studi laurenziani*. Florence: Olschki Editore.

———. 1965b. "La tradizione manoscritta dell' 'Uccellagione di starne.'" *Rinascimento* 5:51–85.

———, ed. 1966. *Simposio*. Florence: Olschki Editore.

Medici, Lorenzo de'. For general editions of his literary works, see Bigi 1965, Carducci, Castaldo, Cavalli, Chastel, Maier 1969, Simioni, and Stange.

———. *Ambra*. See Bessi 1986.

———. 1927. *Canzoni scandalose*. Niguarda: Industria graf. niguardese.

———. *Canzoniere*. See Orvieto 1984.

———. 1977–81. *Lettere*. Ed. N. Rubinstein and R. Fubini. 4 vols. Florence: Giunti-Barbera.

———. *La Nencia da Barberino*. See Bessi 1982.

———. *La rappresentazione di S. Giovanni e Paolo*. See Doglio.

———. *Selve d'amore*. See Castagnola.

———. *Simposio*. See Martelli 1966.

———. *Uccellagione di starne*. See Chiari and Martelli 1965b.

Migliorini, B., and T. Gwynfor Griffith. 1984. *The Italian Language*. London: Faber and Faber.

Mutini, C., ed. 1970. *La cultura a Firenze al tempo di Lorenzo il Magnifico*. Bologna: Zanichelli.

Oliva, Carlo, ed. 1978. *Poesia italiana del Quattrocento*. Milan: Garzanti.

Orvieto, Paolo. 1976. *Lorenzo de' Medici*. Florence: La Nuova Italia.

———, ed. 1984. *Canzoniere*. Milan: Arnoldo Mondadori Editore.

Palmarocchi, Roberto. 1941. *Lorenzo de' Medici*. Turin: UTET.

Poliziano, Angelo. 1979. *The Stanze*. Trans. D. Quint. Amherst: University of Massachusetts Press.

Pound, Ezra. 1970. *The Cantos*. New York: New Directions.

Rochon, André. 1963. *La jeunesse de Laurent de Medicis (1449–1478)*. Paris: Les Belles Lettres.

Roscoe, William. 1883 (1795). *Life of Lorenzo de' Medici, called The Magnificent*. London: George Routledge and Sons.

Ross, Janet, trans. 1911. *Lives of the Early Medici as told in their correspondence*. Boston: R. G. Badger.

Rubinstein, Nicolai. 1971. *Il governo di Firenze sotto i Medici (1434–1494)*. Florence: La Nuova Italia.

Schulz, Juergen. 1975. "Michelangelo's Unfinished Works." *Art Bulletin* 57:366–73.

Simioni, Attilio, ed. 1939 (1913). *Opere*. 2 vols. Bari: G. Laterza.

Spongano, Raffaele. 1964. *Due saggi sull' Umanesimo*. Florence: Sansoni.

Stange, Carl, trans. 1940. *Lorenzo il Magnifico: Dichtungen*. 2 vols. Bremen: Hauschild.

Sturm, Sara. 1974. *Lorenzo de' Medici*. New York: Twayne.

Summers, David. 1981. *Michelangelo and the Language of Art*. Princeton, N.J.: Princeton University Press.

Symonds, John Addington. 1964 (1881). *Renaissance in Italy: Italian Literature*. Part 1. New York: Capricorn Books.

Tateo, Francesco. 1972. *Lorenzo de' Medici e Angelo Poliziano*. Bari: Laterza.

Tolnay, Charles de. 1964. *The Art and Thought of Michelangelo*. Trans. N. Buranelli. New York: Pantheon Books.

Valency, M., and H. Levtow, eds. 1960. *The Palace of Pleasure: An Anthology of the Novella*. New York: Capricorn Books.

Varese, Claudio, ed. 1955. *Prosatori volgari del Quattrocento*. Milan and Naples: Ricciardi.

Vossler, Karl. 1900. *Italienische Literaturgeschichte*. Leipzig: G. J. Goschen.

Wadsworth, James B. 1952. "Landino's *Disputationes Camaldulenses*, Ficino's *De Felicitate*, and *L'Altercazione* of Lorenzo de' Medici." *Modern Philology* 50:23–31.

Wind, Edgar. 1958. *Pagan Mysteries in the Renaissance*. New Haven: Yale University Press.

Zanato, T. 1979. *Saggio sul 'Comento' di Lorenzo de' Medici*. Florence: Olschki.

www.ingramcontent.com/pod-product-compliance
Lightning Source LLC
Chambersburg PA
CBHW030647110726
47901CB00002B/598